Deaf Hearing Boy

(Left to right) Richard C. Miller, Jr., and Robert H. Miller, 1943

Deaf Hearing Boy

A Memoir

R. H. Miller

Gallaudet University Press
Washington, D.C.

Deaf Lives
A Series Edited by Brenda Jo Brueggemann

Gallaudet University Press
Washington, D.C. 20002
http://gupress.gallaudet.edu

© 2004 by Gallaudet University
All rights reserved
Published in 2004
Printed in the United States of America

*Interior page design and composition
by Stephen Tiano Page Design & Production*

Library of Congress Cataloging-in-Publication Data

Miller, R. H. (Robert Henry), 1938-
   Deaf hearing boy : a memoir / R.H. Miller.
   p. cm. -- (Deaf lives)
   ISBN 1-56368-305-9 (pbk. : alk. paper)
   1. Miller, R. H. (Robert Henry), 1938- 2. Children of deaf
parents--United States--Biography. I. Title. II. Series.

HQ759.912.M55 2004
306.874'087'2--dc22   2004047078

⊗ The paper used in this publication meets the minimum
requirements of American National Standard for Information
Sciences— Permanence of Paper for Printed Library Materials,
ANSI Z39.48-1984.

To my daughters
Becky, Rachel, Amy

Contents

Foreword

And, even though I don't know you, I know you. You know what it's like. Partly, I don't have to do so much explaining. But I guess, it's also that I can trust you. Because it's not just my family we are talking about, it's yours too.

—A CODA informant in Paul Preston's
Mother Father Deaf: Living Between Sound and Silence

BOB MILLER AND I have never met. Yet I know Bob Miller as if he were a lifelong friend. Twenty pages into his memoir, I am looking into the mirror. It is amazing to me that this can be true. His life is my life. Not in all the details but in the general life experiences. It is in our shared life experiences that the rubber hits the road for CODAs (Children of Deaf Adults). Our experiences train us to be very private people. In the years before I was thirty, I rarely told anyone I didn't know well that my parents were Deaf and only then if it was "forced out" of me. It is not that I wasn't proud of my parents, I just couldn't handle the ignorance of the world in general or the hypocrisy of those who "work with the Deaf" or who were human service professionals. For CODAs the world is neither as we would like nor as people think they see it. The pieces don't always fit as expected. Yet, the world continues on. The Hearing world, in particular, continues on not only in ignorance but with a plantation mentality. The Hearing world believes that Deaf people should want what the Hearing world wants for them: to hear, to be hearing, to act hearing. The Deaf world knows this but knows it cannot and will not be what the Hearing world wants. The people of the Deaf world, our parents—mine and Bob Miller's—have learned how to live in the Hearing world in order to survive. Bob and I grew up in between these two worlds.

Bob Miller, myself, and thousands of other CODAs are the children of the Deaf in the Deaf world. We developed survival techniques as we learned about the Hearing world. We have learned about the Hearing world in at least three ways. First, we learned from our Deaf parents and their Deaf friends from the cultural perspective of the Deaf world. Second, we learned from our CODA friends, the children of our parents' friends, who were older in age and wiser in amassing strategies for handling what they learned from both the Deaf and Hearing worlds. What CODAs passed on was not always accurate but it was information we could operate from. This process was uncannily similar to how Deaf children who grew up in residential schools learned from their peers. In our lives, many good and bad decisions were made based on the immediate moment and not on vast resources of previously acquired information. Third, we learned how to function through our interactions with the Hearing world. We learned what Hearing people thought of our parents: "Oh, how sad!" "Oh, it must be so hard." We learned that we, as CODAs, had a problem or carried some kind of burden because our parents were Deaf. Hearing people rarely ever understood when they encountered our Deaf parents. It's as if the only fact of importance was that they were Deaf. Their hearing loss overshadowed all things and became the measure of their lives instead of what they were as people. As very young children, we often were put in a position of having to explain both our lives and our Deaf parents' lives, and then live our lives under confusing misinformation from both worlds.

We learned, for example, about how our parents are viewed especially within our extended family. More than 90 percent of Deaf people have Hearing parents and then again, 90 percent of Deaf parents have Hearing children. This means that the Hearing children whose mothers and fathers are Deaf do not usually have an older generation of experts who can assist and advise them early in their lives about how the world is structured and what to expect from people who aren't Deaf. The early lives of CODAs parallel those of the children of immigrants whose parents have been cut off from their relatives and elders. Like these immigrant parents, Deaf people gather together in common bondage and this creates the Deaf world. The bonding is not in physical spaces like the geographical areas or city precincts often shared by immigrants, but rather in mental spaces achieved through cultural and social companionship.

Our Deaf parents of the 1940s, 1950s, and 1960s had a common upbringing in most cases. The last thirty years, however, have brought tremendous changes in the educational system. Deaf adults of today usually have been schooled in either a mainstream setting where they went to school with Hearing students or in other types of programming where they went to Hearing schools but were educated in separate classes with other Deaf peers. This generation of Deaf adults has been "tutored" or "educated" by the Hearing world. They learned to exist in the world through their schooling experiences.

We might expect then that, given the differences in generations of Deaf parents, today's CODAs would have different experiences growing up. As the chairman of the CODA scholarship committee, I read hundreds of essays by CODAs between the ages of seventeen and forty. This would put their parents in the latest generation of Deaf people (those born in the late-60s and 70s). With all the technological advances and changes in laws pertaining to Deaf issues we might think that the lives of CODAs and Deaf people should be much improved compared to my generation and that of Bob Miller's. Yet, in the writings of many young CODAs the themes and the experiences are the same. This is because most of the issues that create their experiences stem from the interaction between their Deaf parents and the Hearing world. The issues of interpreting, misunderstanding what hearing loss means, outright prejudice, hidden prejudices, discrimination, and negative statements made about our parents are still the main themes of this new generation. This is why the heritage of CODAs and Deaf people are one generation thick. Once our parents are gone and their grandchildren are grown, the transmission of Deaf culture, Deaf identity, and the Deaf language are history. Each Deaf generation has to recreate, reinvent, and reimplement its coping strategies, its awareness, its ability to interact, and its ability to survive. Stories like Bob Miller's function as lodestars for those who cannot explain why or how things have happened to them. Miller's is a story for the masses but is also a guide to survival for Deaf parents and especially their Hearing children.

Because Miller's experience was in the 1940s and 50s, we would expect it to be different in the generations of CODAs today. Yet, I believe his experience is repeated in every generation of CODAs. It must be true that the more things change the more they stay the same. Even though today's Deaf parents are more likely to graduate from a local public school and live with their Hearing parents rather than attend a residential school for the Deaf, the life experiences are not greatly different. Slightly more than 55 percent will have been exposed to a signed language while they were in school while approximately

40 percent will continue to be orally educated. While the educational wars between Signed Language and oral methods continue on, more than 90 percent of all graduates, no matter what program they attended, will become part of the Deaf community. They will constitute the Deaf world. They will quite likely marry other Deaf adults and they will more than likely have Hearing children. These Hearing children will repeat the experiences of Bob Miller. For his story is not unique, it is only hidden. Hidden in the corners of society where most people fear to tread. Hidden because of the way our parents continue to be treated.

It is true that history repeats itself. Even with all the new technology the Deaf of today still have great difficulty getting the Hearing world to understand that they are equals. Bob Miller's is a story about equality, about people who took care of themselves, and even took care of their own (Hearing) parents. It is a story about people who raised four children. This is a story about people who persevered in the face of prejudice, discrimination, and outright thievery. This is a story about participant witnesses: the children of Deaf people.

Most of the Deaf people in this world have Hearing children who grew up and witnessed all their parents' trials and tribulations. The irony is that these parents are part of a thriving, warm, and supportive community that the Hearing world remains relatively ignorant of. CODAs grow up in a community and world quietly existing right at the feet of the Hearing world.

Our quest as CODA children coming of age was to learn to separate ourselves from our parents, the Deaf world, and the protection it may have offered. As adults most of us entered the Hearing world and left the Deaf world behind. This separation was no easy task. There are CODA memoirs, mostly from women, who describe this separation from family. Miller's memoir however presents itself from

the male perspective. It is not much different than the female perspective: You feel guilty just because you want to leave, because the
demands can be overwhelming. You feel guilty when you don't leave
and the demands and stresses overtake your life. You feel guilty when
you leave because you are not sure what effect this may have on your
parents. Many times, because of our age at the time of these decisions, we don't know what to do and can be overwhelmed by this
real feeling of powerlessness. Handling the huge chore of managing
the Hearing and Deaf worlds is not part of the typical developmen-
tal process for children, and some CODAs begin taking on this task
as young as five or six years old. This process is clearly laid out in
Miller's memoir. To truly understand the emotions, the feelings, the
experiences and reasons behind this memoir, the Hearing reader
must try to look at themselves from the perspective of Deaf people.
How many Deaf people have you met? How many of them were
parents? How many CODAs have you met and interacted with?
What do we really know about growing up in a Deaf family? In
truth, many readers will have met more CODAs than they realize.

Deaf people are rare, it is true, but the real issue isn't numbers, it
is the attitudes that society develops toward Deaf people. In general,
Hearing people believe that to be Deaf is to be unable to communicate and as a result Deaf people are seen as atypical or somehow less
than Hearing people. There is no denying this fact and it is displayed
whenever CODAs interact with Hearing people in the presence of
their parents. As children, CODAs are exposed to this in myriad ways,
but their role as interpreters maximizes exposure to the values and
attitudes of the Hearing world.

Who are the outsiders in the world of CODAs and their Deaf
parents? The answer might surprise even many of us who are on the
inside. Miller's memoir presents some insights into what extended

family members think about their Deaf sons, daughters, brothers, and sisters and what those Deaf family members think about their Hearing relatives. This memoir opens up a discussion about the extended family and how much Hearing parents know about their own Deaf children. It is not a subject often explored by CODAs as we tend to keep our discussions of relationships confined to those with our Deaf parents. Sometimes remembering how our grandparents, aunts, and uncles treated our parents can be very painful.

It is a tribute to most CODAs that we survived as psychological wholes. It is a tribute that we grow up and realize who our parents are and what hardships they have endured to see that we did grow up. We are a reflection of them. Strong, caretaking survivors who will pass on to our own children the tremendous assets that our parents' have passed on to us.

In Bob Miller's memoir a path many CODAs have taken—perhaps not in the same steps but in the same woods—is presented as one of survival, love, and independence. Many of us are beginning to tell our stories and the world is beginning to see (pun intended) our parents and us in a different light. For our stories are as much about our parents as they are about ourselves. The future is our children, be they Deaf or Hearing.

This book is in the line of other CODA memoirs from Lou Ann Walker (1987) to Lennard Davis (2000). Each memoir shares the secrets we all hold as each succeeding text reveals another layer of experience. Bob Miller takes us one step further into exposing who we are, how we have gotten here, and I hope for the next generation of CODAs how they too might get there.

Robert J. Hoffmeister

Acknowledgments

I am deeply grateful to Robert Hoffmeister for his heartfelt and authoritative commentary on my book. I particularly value his insights into my experience as it relates to Deaf people today. It is a great compliment to my family for us to know that our lives together have contributed toward an understanding of the complex interplay between Deaf parents and Hearing children, and those families' place in the community at large.

I cannot begin to express how important Lennard Davis's *My Sense of Silence* and Lou Ann Walker's *A Loss for Words* have been in helping me understand so many of my experiences. Walker's touching portrayals of both conflicted and tender moments with her parents prodded me to recall similar moments with my mother and father. Although Davis's background and that of his parents are vastly different from my parents' and mine, his recollections always resonate strongly with me. Thanks also to Gerald Davis, whose introduction to his parents' letters, *Shall I Say a Kiss?*, made me appreciate the experience of the older (in my case, oldest) child with his parents.

To the many writers and scholars of Deaf life and culture I am deeply indebted: Paul Preston, Oliver Sacks, Harlan Lane, Brenda Jo

Brueggemann, Carol Padden and Tom Humphries, Robert Hoffmeister, Leah Hager Cohen, Ruth Sidransky, Douglas C. Baynton.

Through his skillful criticism, my friend and colleague Jeff Skinner made it possible for me to write the book I wanted to write, and I thank him deeply. To Susan Hall I am indebted for many writing suggestions throughout the book. To my agent Linda Roghaar I extend thanks for many encouragements, for her professional expertise, and for suggesting the title of this book.

A second thanks goes to my editor Brenda Brueggemann. I am deeply indebted to her for her incisive criticism, many encouragements, and abiding confidence in this book as well as for her helping me say the things I needed to say.

I am grateful to Ivey Pittle Wallace and Deirdre Mullervy of the Gallaudet University Press for their many sound editorial judgments and professional assistance.

To my brother Dick I am indebted for his sensitive, sympathetic reading of an early draft, for that hidden life we shared, and for his tolerating the many times I took my frustrations out on him. In many ways, our parents' deafness created conflicts between us, but in many other ways it brought us closer together.

I owe so much to my wife Diane, who needs no explanations from me, as she has shared the joy and the pain of my experience over forty-four years of confidences with her. I am deeply in her debt for her patience and understanding.

THE FAMILIES

(Principal figures in the book are in bold type.)

Henry and Amy Miller Family

Henry G. Miller, d. 1928 = **Amy G. Font**, d. 1973 = Seth M. Shank, d. 1930 = **Lloyd C. Newton**, d. 1956

Hilda, d. 1908   Lester W., d. 2002   **Richard C.**

Arthur and Ora Sowers Family

Arthur Sowers, d. 1971 = Ora Henning, d. 1967

Eleanor (Householder)   Dorothy (Chaplin), d. 2002   Jean (Bentz, Steyer)

Richard and Elizabeth Miller Family

Elizabeth J. (Miller)

Richard Carl Miller = Elizabeth Jane Sowers

ROBERT H., b. 1938   Richard C., Jr., b. 1940   Arthur R., b. 1945   John A., 1947–2002

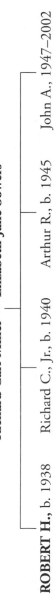

Introduction

Out of this silence yet I picked a welcome,
And in the modesty of fearful duty
I read as much as from the rattling tongue
Of saucy and audacious eloquence.
—*A Midsummer Night's Dream,* 5.1.100–103

This story follows my years with my Deaf parents from my birth in 1938 until my departure for college in 1956, with a final chapter by way of bringing to a close my long association with them over their eighty-plus years of life. I hope it will help my daughters understand what my early life was like as they come to know better the unusual relationship that existed between me and my parents, my parents and their grandparents, and me and my grandparents. I hope, too, that, in some small way, my experiences will assist students of the Deaf community so they can understand more clearly the tensions that exist between Deaf parents and their Hearing children and so they in turn will be better able to recognize the special needs of these children and their parents.

My story includes revelations, confessions, and resurrections of events long dead, and some of them will prove embarrassing and hurtful to my parents and my family. I know that friends and relatives will be dismayed by how I portray some of the actions and attitudes of my grandparents, who were considered "good Christian people" and pillars of the community. I can only say I have tried to present a truthful account, one that honors my subjects but does not shirk its duty to be honest to myself. For any proverbial closeted skeletons that may be rattled here, I am regretful, but my intention, like that of the famous French essayist, Michel de Montaigne, has been to write an honest book.

The uniqueness of my experience with my parents is twofold. First, it stems from my family's nomadic journey from the farm to the city in late 1942 and then back to the farm again at the close of 1949. It also concerns the deprivations we suffered when we had to leave the city, where my parents had depended on a large and flourishing Deaf community for social contact and support. The change was hard for my father to make, but it was devastating to my mother, who thrived on the gregarious life the city provided her as a Deaf person.

Second, the uniqueness of this experience has to do with the tension between my parents and me and between them and my grandparents as well as with the chasm that separated their Deaf world from the Hearing world of Grandma Amy and Grandpa Lloyd Newton. For much of my childhood and adolescence, we shared a house, a farm, and a livelihood with my grandparents. This family construct constitutes Paul Preston's H-D-H schema (Hearing-Deaf-Hearing, referring to the difference in three generations: Hearing grandparents, Deaf parents, and Hearing children) as he describes it in his book, *Mother Father Deaf*.[1] In this construct, the Hearing grandparents and Hearing grandchildren inevitably are drawn into a complex relationship

---

1. Cambridge, Mass.: Harvard University Press, 1994.

that both tries to privilege the prerogatives of the Deaf parents and inevitably in various ways undermines them, as it did in my childhood. Because I was so accustomed to witnessing my parents being treated by other Hearing people as somehow mentally deficient, that is, "deaf and dumb" (and the "dumb" did not necessarily signify being mute), I really didn't see anything out of the ordinary in the way my grand-parents treated them until I was about fifteen and old enough to understand how my parents would never in my grandparents' eyes be quite normal.

Although Lloyd Newton was really my stepgrandfather, I refer to him as Grandpa Lloyd because he was the only paternal grandfather I ever knew; my grandfather Miller died more than ten years before I was born. The portraits I paint here of my paternal grandparents show only a part of my life with them as they dealt with my parents, who could be difficult. My grandparents could be distant, patronizing, and distrustful. My grandmother's behavior was quite different from what was usually the practice among Deaf people, who displayed affec-tion openly, exuberantly, and frequently, but we were caught between two cultures—one Hearing-midwestern and the other Deaf. Ohio farm families were not given to displays of affection under any circum-stances, except perhaps for weddings and funerals. My grandfather's association with my dad, as a stepfather who had married my dad's mother when Dad was fourteen, was almost nonexistent, which is how I portray it in these pages.

In spite of their midwestern reticence, my grandparents' feelings toward me were open and very giving, but the price of that affection was costly to me in the damage it did to my relations with my parents, and I bear some of the blame for it. Had I not been looking for an alternative Hearing family for myself, I might have avoided this conflict. On the other hand, this search has defined my life, and I have always accepted that fact. As a child who was "gifted," I found myself caught in a war of affection between my parents and my grandparents, and only now can I fully understand how harmful it was to us all. I loved my grandparents for all they did for me because, in many ways, they made possible the life I have, but they and I often participated in a conspiracy to usurp the rightful domain of my parents. Initially I was a willing conspirator in this deception, but over time, I began to see through my grandparents' attitude. Toward the end of my teen years, I found myself in deep conflict with them.

Our extended family also had the misfortune to participate in a cataclysmic event, the death of the family farm. In that part of the Midwest, many families eked out a living for themselves on small farms of anywhere from 150 to 350 acres. Our two farms, one of about 110 acres and the other of a little less than 40 acres, even when put together ranked among the smallest of the small farms. As my parents struggled with the economics of trying to live a life of the past in the present, especially at a time when the American family was undergoing tremendous change, it became all too obvious that something would have to give. My grandparents were living in that past, holding on to every dime they could save, putting almost nothing back into the farm, finding themselves unable to respond to the crushing demands my parents had to deal with. In 1953, this farming life finally came to an end when my father and my grandfather sold all their livestock and farm equipment, and my grandparents rented the farm out to a local, high-volume farmer. Until recently I cherished idyllic memories of that earlier existence, but writing this book has brought me around sharply, and now I recognize the poverty and enslavement of that life for what it was. It had its romantic moments, but by and large, it was a life of continual hard work and continual want.

Because my parents kept some barriers between their children and their world, linguistically and otherwise, I was always treated as an outsider in any Deaf context. My parents seemed to feel that too close an association with Deaf culture would prevent me from finding my place in the Hearing world. Any Hearing person who attempted to "cross over" was immediately suspect. Swear words and words having to do with sex we learned from our Deaf and Hearing CODA (children of Deaf adults) peers, and my parents were horrified by any lore of that nature that we happened to acquire. Likewise, they never passed on to us any gossip or accounts of scandal that touched the Deaf community, even though that sort of information must have been plentiful.

At my parents' school, both the teaching and learning of ASL (American Sign Language) were forbidden. Instead, the teachers emphasized speechreading, or the "oral method" (sometimes referred to as "oralism"), as a form of mainstreaming the children, or of teaching them to live in a Hearing world, and no effort was made to encourage their Hearing parents to learn to sign with their children. If anything, it was discouraged, and both sets of my grandparents labored at exaggerated efforts to communicate orally with their children. When speechreading failed, Grandma Sowers, my mother's mother, would fall back on her primitive knowledge of ASL while Grandma Amy would pull out her ever-present pad and pencil. Deaf children actually learned ASL from the older students at the school and grew up using a tolerated but taboo language.

With respect to my own life, I never thought much about what might have been. I had a troubled but rewarding childhood and adolescence. In my account of my early life, I have tried to describe something of the perspective I had as a child growing up—to try to create some feeling for the tension, the fear, the awe of living simultaneously in the world of the Deaf and the Hearing. Much of what I have to say as an adult I have tried to reserve to the part of the book about my adulthood, especially the last chapter and Afterword.

My mother was a pusher, extremely ambitious for me, the Great Deaf Hope, a little too quick with the back of the hand, perhaps, and often unable to control her volatile temper. In her lighter moments, she was very much a prototype of Lois, the mother in the television sitcom *Malcolm in the Middle*, hurling orders right and left, desperately trying to keep her four male charges under some semblance of control, and yet through it all, she exuded a vitality and intense sense of purpose. Quite often, she exercised phenomenally poor judgment and acted with her heart rather than her head. She and I engaged in a battle of emotions for most of my adolescent life. We had a love-hate relationship that would explode into verbal fireworks day in and day out. And yet I always felt close to my mother, even at points in my life when I knew that we had let each other down. In adulthood, we have grown closer together as she has taken pride in my achievements and has bonded with my wife and daughters.

My father has always been a puzzle to me and I think to my brothers as well. Because of our close contact on the farm everyday, as we worked side by side, we had plenty of opportunity to get to know each other well. Deafened by meningitis at eighteen months and fatherless at ten, my father had every reason to withdraw into himself. I don't think I have ever really understood him, but it was never much of an issue as I was growing up because, at that time, fathers generally tended to be remote, masterly, authoritative figures. His approach to us four boys was to leave the usual discipline and decision making to my mother and to intervene only in crises, when he had no trouble making his authority stick. He was a gifted man, and his quickness of mind was a constant surprise to my grandfather and others with whom he worked. He was very bright and genuinely caring, but often, he tended to be aloof, distant from his sons.

My story is also about a marriage that held together against almost insurmountable obstacles created by society and, yes, by the two people bound to each other by it. As a child, I had little appreciation for and, in fact, little awareness of the heroic struggle my parents had to mount just to survive and the extent to which for them there seemed to be no way out of this commitment that they had made quite naïvely when they were still teenagers. One impetuous effort to break out of the marriage produced only a momentary breach and then a hurried reconciliation. And subsequent years of the marriage showed to the world a couple who had to struggle to make a life not only for themselves within the marriage but also for their four sons, whose needs taxed them to their limit. Yet they survived it all more successfully in many ways than did some of their Hearing siblings.

Almost all the information I present here is drawn from memory, not a prodigious one but a fairly competent one. Where it has been in conflict with others' memories, especially those of my parents, I have chosen to rely on my own, in keeping with the nature of this book as a memoir, not a history. Although I cannot vouch for the verbatim accuracy of conversations, I have made every effort to be as faithful as I can to my recollection of those scenes in my life. I expect that my family will have good reason to agree with the truth of Erasmus's adage, "*Odi memorem compotorem*," "I hate a drinking buddy with a good memory," especially if it were modified to "I hate a nosy kid with a good memory."

The title of the book reflects the truth that, in the words of the English essayist Sir Thomas Browne, I lived "in divided and distinguished worlds"—the world of Deaf people and of Hearing people—and absorbed cultural qualities of both. Particularly in matters of language, I found myself drawn to ASL (American Sign Language), which I had learned from birth, and poor as my mastery of it is today, I consider it my first language. It has been perhaps more a part of my process of linguistic maturation than it is of many Deaf people who pick up ASL later in life, usually in school, when they begin to associate with other Deaf children. As I became a user of spoken English, I was equally drawn to that language, and its study has become my lifelong occupation.

I add two comments by way of explanation. First, when I say I "said" this or that to my parents or they "told" me something, understand that I always mean expressed in ASL or in "home signing," a personal sign language that many Deaf parents rely on when communicating with their Hearing children. For us, home signs consisted of a combination of ASL, fingerspelling, and efforts by my

Newton farmhouse, 1956, where our family lived, 1940–42, 1950–73. We occupied the left side of the house, the porch side.

parents to converse with us orally. Almost all Deaf people have perfect vocal ability, but because they cannot hear the sound of the human voice, they lack the paradigms of speech and consequently produce nonnormal vocalization patterns. Hence, my mother's voice always sounded high and screechy whereas my dad's guttural voice sounded closer to the norm because he had the advantage of being able to hear for eighteen months. Second, in most cases, I have converted ASL conversations into Standard English. I also try to follow the accepted convention of using the lowercase "deaf" to denote matters related to hearing deficiency and the uppercase "Deaf" to refer to Deafness as a cultural phenomenon. The same convention applies also to the use of the word *hearing*.

Finally, although I have been committed to creating an honest account, I have made one exception. In a few instances, for reasons of privacy, I have used pseudonyms rather than actual names.

1

Early Life (1938–1942)

I AM BORN in a small hospital in Defiance, Ohio, at 11:45 in the morning on Wednesday, August 10, 1938, on the day between the birthdays of my mother and her mother. But I am really not to be the hero of my story. Instead, like Adam and Eve in John Milton's *Paradise Lost*, my parents would become the heroes, as they, "hand in hand, with wandering steps and slow," made their solitary way through the Hearing world, burdened by their deafness as our original parents were by original sin.

My birth name "Bobby Henry" I have never used since I started school, where I was immediately re-christened "Robert" by my Hearing teachers. It was a victory for my grandparents, all four of them, who had tried in vain to explain to my parents that "Bobby" was not a proper name for a child. Of course, had they lived a little farther to the south, where I live now, they would have found it perfectly acceptable, if not preferred. My parents, however, were proud and determined people. They would have none of it, and I have never been inclined to change it officially. If I ever run for public office here in Kentucky, maybe I'll resurrect the name "Bobby." (My parents went through a similar hassle naming my youngest brother when a hospital official insisted his name should be "John Adams Miller," after our second president, rather than "John Adam," his middle name chosen in memory of our great-grandfather Adam Miller.)

Luke 2:23 tells us that "every male child that openeth the womb shall be holy to the Lord," and in many ways, I believe I was blessed, but my birth caused tremendous anxiety in the families of my parents. The inevitable questions were How can we cope with another deaf child in the family? and Can these Deaf kids bring up a deaf child (at my birth my mother was a day older than twenty, my dad some nine months older)? Everyone expected me to be born deaf. Both sets of parents thought their Deaf son and Deaf daughter's marriage would produce deaf children, even though in my parents' case, one of the partners was not prenatally deaf. My dad became deaf at the age of eighteen months from spinal meningitis, a fact that would place the odds of Mom's bearing a deaf child at being no greater than those for the population at large.

My parents dropped out of school and eloped by train to Indiana, where the consent laws for marriage were more liberal than they were in Ohio. My mother boarded the train in Fostoria, my dad in Defiance, and they detrained in Auburn, where they were married on July 31, 1936, an act both brave and foolish. Their parents greeted the marriage with shock because it meant neither Mom nor Dad would finish school. Dad had no way of supporting Mom. He had no job, no high school diploma, no training whatever, and he was Deaf. Mom's mother was horrified that her daughter might be pregnant and asked her whether she was. Mom told her no, that she and Dad just wanted to be together.

So with no pregnancy in sight for the moment, the demon of producing "deformed" children could be stayed. But, more than a year later, my parents would have foolishly created a pregnancy and all the problems that were sure to come with it. And they would go on to create three more, and each one would produce a hearing child, much to the amazement of my grandparents. Many years later, when I was in high school, my Grandmother Sowers mentioned to me how lucky my parents were to have had all hearing children. Even though I wasn't really informed on the topic then, I knew from my own contact with the Deaf community that they had not been "lucky." In fact, they were the norm. I said to her, "Grandma, most

Elizabeth Sowers and Richard Miller, at the Ohio State School for the Deaf, April 1936, three months before they eloped.

deaf parents have hearing children." She was stunned and perplexed because she and her hearing husband had produced not one but two deaf babies.

During the years I was growing up, my grandparents always doubted that my parents could be successful parents. My dad's mother, my Grandma Amy Newton, fretted over my mother's ability to handle her responsibilities. Yet my grandmother, the victim of a terrible irony, would shortly be the one who was caring for me when I lost the sight in my right eye. As far as their parents were concerned, my parents had shamed the families and defied scientific opinion by irresponsibly eloping and getting married. Mom was seventeen, soon to be eighteen; Dad was eighteen already.

Years later, my prospective mother-in-law had the courage to tell me up front that she was concerned that if her daughter and I were to marry, her daughter would bear deaf children. It was an attitude, a prejudice that my brothers and I often confronted in dating. I swallowed my rage and patiently explained to her that the odds of that happening were no greater for us than for any married couple because my father had not been born deaf. Nevertheless, I think that, deep down, she was unconvinced until our first child was born. More hurtful to me, however, was the feeling I couldn't shake, that she believed Deaf people were somehow subnormal. However, after our marriage, as the years went by, my in-laws became deeply attached to my parents.

Now that scientific research has identified many of the genetic factors in deafness, we can understand better the complexities of prenatal deafness. Besides, what better parent to bring up a deaf child than someone who has been reared by Deaf parents? For my wife and me, it would have been a burden, but a burden lovingly accepted. That perspective is one shared widely by people immersed in Deaf culture, either CODAs or Deaf people themselves, who can appreciate the good things of that life. As my own children have thought about the possibility of having a deaf child, I've tried to share that perspective with them. Yet after each of our children was born, I did what Lennard Davis did. Davis, also a CODA and a professor, is the author of a fine book on his Deaf parents, *My Sense of Silence*. Like him, I rattled my keys over my kids' heads, just to be sure.

At the time I was born, my parents lived in No. 1 Cottage, one of three small cottages across the road from the dairy farm owned by my grandparents, south of Defiance on State Route 111. The cottages, now razed, sat on the northwest bank of the Auglaize River. No. 1 Cottage was a tiny, four-room affair: kitchen, "front" room, two very small bedrooms, and an enclosed mud porch with a hand pump in one corner on the back of the house. The outdoor toilet stood about fifty feet away, at the edge of a steep drop-off along the riverbank, looking as if at any moment it would slide into the river. I think sometime in the '50s it did finally get sliced off from the shore during ice-out. Luckily it wasn't occupied. My grandparents lived directly across the highway in the old Newton farmhouse, built in the late nineteenth century. It was a neat white wood clapboard house with two large pine trees in front of it, and its green sheet metal roof would clatter loudly when it rained. The sound was one I always loved to hear on warm summer nights as I lay in bed, separated from the metal panels by only lath and plaster.

I am very small, about a year old. Grandma Amy comes over to the little cottage to check on things, as she has a habit of doing because she is always afraid that I might be in some danger and my parents won't be able to hear me.

No. 1 Cottage, 1938, where we first lived, across the road (State Route 111) from the Newton farmhouse. In the background is the Auglaize River.

I am sitting perilously close to the edge of the counter, beside the kitchen pump, one of those small pumps that are bolted to wood surfaces, and am eating canned peaches from a jar, dipping my hand into the jar and stuffing the peach slices in my mouth. Juice runs down my chin onto my little undershirt, I am a sticky mess, and of course, Grandma disapproves.

Mom turns to Dad and signs something to him, my eyes all the time watching, and I begin screaming and throwing a huge tantrum. Dad grabs me to keep me from falling from my perch.

Grandma asks Mom what has happened and Mom replies, "Oh, I told Richard it is time to get Bobby cleaned up and put to bed."

So I begin my life as a Deaf child who can hear, and ASL is my first language. I begin the journey from one culture to another, but I never really leave my Deafness behind, and at points in my life I am drawn back to it, with shocks of recognition along the way.

To the east of the farmhouse were garages, brooder houses (for raising young chicks), a large chicken coop, two working gardens, tool
shed, milk house, a large dairy barn with bullpen and loafing shed
and silo, then a granary with pigpen, and beyond that the "horse barn"
(which had no horses in my time because tractors had replaced them)
and a couple more machinery sheds. Beyond the buildings were a
large pasture, Five Mile Creek, and fields of corn, oats, and hay. The
farm was a subsistence farm, intended to provide all the needs of the
family, with a profit from the dairy operation supplying a comfortable
cash flow. In its day, it had been one of the showpieces of Defiance
County and its dairy herd one of the finest in the state, but it had
fallen on hard times during the tenure of my stepgrandfather's father,
who had depleted the cash savings of the farm. To my Grandpa
Lloyd's misfortune, his first marriage had been childless, a tragedy for
any farm family, which depends on the combined labor of the entire
family, especially of the sons. Later in his life, because of severe
lameness from a form of arthritis, he was unable to do any serious
work on the farm and came to depend on a series of "hired men"
and their families to run the farm, one of whom of course was my
father. The families lasted only a few years because he was a hard
man to please and tight with a dollar.

Five miles east-northeast on Route 111 was Defiance, a growing
community of about 6,000 people. The town takes its name from
Fort Defiance, a small fortification built at the confluence of the
Auglaize and Maumee Rivers, which was erected in late July 1794 by
General "Mad Anthony" Wayne during his Indian campaign. Most
of the population of the county was of German Protestant descent,
with a sizeable German Catholic minority. It had only three Deaf

people, my mother and father and a young unmarried daughter of a Hearing family in Defiance. Today, its Deaf population has risen slightly to three couples and several Deaf children of Hearing parents, which shows how unwilling Deaf people are to locate away from urban centers.

Back in the early 1930s, at the School for the Deaf, my mom and dad had gradually moved from an innocent adolescent infatuation with each other into a deeper romantic relationship. There was always a kind of unreal quality to their relationship and to the expectations that went with it. As I was looking through some of their school autograph books, a custom now out of favor, I found inscriptions from their friends about Richard and Elizabeth being "of all the romance in the world." It is a poignant phrase not immediately accessible to the Hearing but one that must have meant to them everything that love could possibly hold. Even in the darkest days of their marriage, they still seemed to share a kind of grade-school innocence in their affection for each other.

They had met at the Ohio State School for the Deaf in Columbus as children and had crushes on each other from grade school years into high school. One of the school buildings they attended still stands, but it has been converted into a state office building. The school grounds, downtown behind the city library, have been converted into a lovely topiary garden representing Georges Seurat's famous pointillist painting, *Sunday on the Island of the Grande Jatte.* At that time, the school had an enrollment of more than 300 pupils. In the 1950s, a new school for Deaf students was built on the north side of Columbus. Today, it enrolls only about 150, reflecting the trend toward mainstreaming. Dad had been sent off to school from his parents' farm in Paulding County. Mom had begun her schooling at the Findlay School for the Deaf, near her parents' home in the small town of Fostoria. Later she moved on to the school in Columbus.

Mom's parents, Arthur and Ora Sowers, had the biological "misfortune" to produce not one but two deaf daughters of the four girls they brought into the world. Mom was the oldest, and she shared her "handicap" with her third sister Dorothy. Grandma Sowers had nothing but love for them and did everything she could to see to their upbringing. Contrary to the pattern found among some hearing parents of deaf children, my mother's mother had an almost smothering interest in the lives of her deaf girls. She did everything she could for them, and they loved her deeply in return. Unfortunately, she never achieved more than a primitive knowledge of ASL. That cultural divide was still too wide for her to cross, although she made a much greater effort to communicate with her daughter than Grandma Amy did with her son.

Just after Mom and Dad are married, Grandma Amy takes her along to the Junction Methodist Church to a quilting bee. Mom, who is a crackerjack seamstress, enjoys the experience immensely.

As they begin work, Grandma pulls out her ever-present pad and pencil to make a suggestion to Mom about her stitching. When she does, all the women begin to scold her for not being able to sign to Mom. Grandma complains that she can't because her arthritis is so bad.

Years later, Mom tells me this story and comments wryly, "She may have had arthritis, but she sure could stitch."

My parents were driven together by a desperate need to find parental affection in their own feelings for each other. My father played father to my mother in many ways, and she played mother to him, and they and their peers at the Deaf school formed a family of their own among themselves to compensate for the family life they never really had. As my parents have grown old and outlived many of their friends, the ones they mourn the most are their class-mates from school.

In the few photos that have survived from his childhood, my father looks like a very lonely boy. He was a bright child, only to have his hearing taken from him by disease and then to be sent away to school at a very young age. Soon, he would lose his father and then a stepfather as his mother sought to provide a secure life for herself and her two sons. Ultimately, my father was able to find a place for his affection in his love for my mother, a love that seemed perfect but would be tested, and for his four sons. My father has always been a private, I think lonely person, but he found a measure of peace in his family and in his Deaf friends.

Of my birth grandfather I know very little. He was a modestly successful farmer with the sonorous name of Henry Gideon Miller (Henry—my middle name and the name of one of my grandsons). His father's family had emigrated as a group in 1863 from the small village of Gächlingen, outside Schaffhausen in the Swiss canton by that name, and had settled near Archbold, Ohio. In 1982, my wife and I spent a beautiful late spring day touring that lovely Swiss village. Eerily, I found in the churchyard cemetery a grave marker for Robert Müller, with the epitaph, "Daheim ist's gut" ("Home 'tis well").

My dad's mother, Amy Grace Font, was born in Hartsburg, Putnam County, and grew up in Gilboa and Junction, the second child in a family of ten children. The Fonts and the Millers lived on farms almost adjacent to each other, so if Dobie Gillis's law that "love is propinquity" is true, then it was perfectly natural that two of the Miller boys would wed two of the Font girls. Amy Grace Font and Henry Gideon Miller were married on June 24, 1904, and had three children,

Lloyd and Amy Newton, my dad's mother and his stepfather (wedding photo?), 1932. Ray's of Defiance, Ohio.

a daughter Hilda, who died in infancy, a son Lester William, and my father Richard Carl.

My grandmother confided to me that she and her husband had no idea how to cope with the deafness that spinal meningitis had inflicted on their little son Richard. Fortunately, they were given information by a relative about a free school for deaf children in Columbus, operated by the state. As soon as he was of age, he was sent there and stayed there, often through summers after the death of his father, until he turned eighteen, when he and my mother eloped. My dad always shared an affectionate bond with his brother Lester, but Lester, several years older than he, was a Hearing person, and Dad saw him only in those summers when he was brought home from the Deaf school. I think also that, as an "accidental Deaf" person, my dad was dissociative in ways that marked him. Even those eighteen months of life as a hearing being acculturated him to a hearing environment and set him apart in subtle ways that he could not fully understand.

The second tragedy in his early life occurred on March 19, 1928, when his father died in his forty-third year. He had suffered for several years from stomach ulcers, and on that late winter afternoon, he succumbed at home to an "obstruction of the bowels," as his death certificate reads.

It is a dark, chilly March night at the Deaf School in Columbus. My father is sound asleep. Suddenly he is awakened by Matron, who summons him, in his pajamas, to the office of the superintendent of the school. He is ushered in and stands there, wrapped in sleep, a confused, bleary-eyed ten-year-old boy.

The Superintendent says to him, slowly, so he can read his lips, "Richard, your mother called. I am sorry to have to tell you your father has died. I am very sorry."

Then Matron takes him back to the room and puts him to bed.

My father told me this story out of the blue one Sunday afternoon. We were making small talk during half time as we watched a football game together. He shared it as if it had been on his mind for years to tell it so it might not be forgotten, and he told it with dignity. I sat silent and couldn't reply. Never in his life had my father confided in me in such an intimate way.

At the School for the Deaf, Richard Miller was a super-bright student and a gifted athlete, active in three sports. He exhibited a talent for drawing, crafting, and creating, and if the opportunities had been there for him, he would have excelled at anything he chose.

After Amy Miller lost her husband Henry, like most women at that time who had two young sons to take care of (one "handicapped," the other a teenager) and no training for the job market, she remarried to a widower twenty-five years older than she—Seth M. Shank, a semiretired schoolteacher and former public official and a person of means and education. Unfortunately, after a little longer than six months of what was a happy marriage, Seth Shank died. Six months of wedded bliss brought Amy Shank the duty of executing Shank's will, a modest inheritance, and the responsibility once more of finding a family situation for herself and her sons.

Now comfortably situated, Amy Shank met a childless widower and dairy farmer from a prominent Defiance County family that had fallen on hard times. Lloyd Charles Newton, the only survivor of two sons, had been a partner with his father on the family farm. The Newtons had acquired prosperous agricultural holdings, among them a dairy farm of some repute and a working dairy. The family originally had come to the United States from Coldstream, Scotland, on the Scots-English border and had a rather cold, calculating view of things, perhaps a reflection of that mode of living they must have experienced in the hostile border country. So the two widowers lived together on the financially teetery farm until the arrival of the well-off widow Amy (Miller) Shank.

Amy had doubts about the marriage because the Newtons were on the brink of bankruptcy. She agreed to the marriage on the condition that half the Newton farm be deeded over to her outright in return for which, apparently, she agreed to advance her future father-in-law and her husband-to-be a substantial amount of money. In effect, she became owner in her own right of half of the farm, and on marrying, she became owner by joint tenancy of the rest. This arrangement seems not to have affected her relationship with Grandpa Lloyd for she deferred to him in all matters having to do with the farm as if he were sole owner. Later, she bought a property in her own name in Paulding County, which was called the "Other Place," a summer retreat of which I have many fond memories, and she depended on Grandpa Lloyd to oversee its management, too.

Elizabeth Sowers, my mother, was spirited, happy, but tormented by problems at school. She lagged; she found her lessons confusing. By the time she had reached seventeen, she knew she would never be able to finish. Over the years, my mother would often marvel at how easily things came to my father and to me, how much we enjoyed reading, which she had to struggle to do. She constantly denigrated her intelligence, which was considerable, and called herself "stupid," using the ASL sign of the clenched fist rapped against the forehead. No matter how much I tried to convince her that her problems were caused by early learning deprivation she always felt inadequate. When, later in life, I told her I had published a couple of books and some scholarly articles, she insisted on having them, and I gave her copies. Shortly after that she said to me, "Bobby, I read your pieces. I didn't understand any of them, but they are wonderful!" And all her Deaf friends who have come to the house have been dragooned into looking at these publications. They are probably my largest audience, perhaps my only dedicated audience, come to think of it.

My mother also was a beautiful, outgoing girl, the daughter of a deeply religious, loving mother and a somewhat distant father, often ill tempered, who kept his four daughters at arm's length. He was a veteran of World War I, and my mother was born in 1918 while he was overseas. He returned to establish his butcher shop, which provided a livelihood for him and his wife until the Great Depression wiped them out and left them barely able to keep their family in food and clothes. As Depression survivors, my Sowers grandparents were scarred by the experience and never fully recovered.

Both my mother's parents had had very hard lives. My grandfather was an abandoned child, a street urchin, who was taken in by a family in Fostoria when he was only four. My grandmother's mother died giving birth to my grandmother, and my grandmother subsequently endured years of abuse from her stepmother. Finally, she was able to escape when, as teenagers, she and her older sister moved out and got their own apartment. They supported themselves working in a cigar factory.

So it was that on or about that first day of August in 1936, my dad and mom, now married, boarded that return train at Auburn and headed back to Fostoria and Mom's parents. Later, after Mom's parents phoned them, Lloyd and Amy Newton made the trip from Defiance to Fostoria where they hoped to convince my parents to have their marriage annulled, but it was no use. The young couple would have none of it. Grandma Amy also tempted Dad with the news that she had cleared the way for him to return to the deaf school (but not Mom, who was expelled) and that, after his senior year, she would send him to Gallaudet University, which of course would have been a marvelous opportunity for my multitalented father. Again, Dad refused.

As Grandma Amy confided to me much later, she was in shock and had no idea what to do with or for the young couple. Finally, with the agreement of her husband of three-plus years and of Mom's parents, she placed them in the small cottage she owned on the river across the road from the farmhouse, and Dad became a tenant farmer in the employ of his stepfather at a paid salary of ten dollars a week and free rent and food from the farm. For the first few years of their

(Left) Elizabeth and Richard Miller, and Bobby, 1938. Elite Studio, Defiance, Ohio.

(Right) Grandma Amy and Bobby, on the front lawn at the farm, 1939.

married life, they had no car because Dad, being handicapped, had to wait until he was twenty-one to qualify for a driver's license.

The newlyweds settled down to housekeeping together, until a little more than two years later when I, their first son Bobby Henry, arrived, and the long honeymoon came to an end. The two years they shared before I was born must have been the most peaceful of their lives. Their dreams had come true; they were there for each other as they had always hoped to be, in the cottage on the river, with no cares, no worries.

On January 25, 1940, my brother Dick (Richard Carl, Jr.) was born at home. That night, a major snowstorm kept Mom from being taken into Defiance to the hospital. Instead, Dad's cousin Velma Keck, who was a nurse, managed to get to the house, and Dick came into the world in true country fashion. Through those early years, he and I formed one of two sibling pairs, as if my brothers Art and John, who were born in 1945 and 1947, made up a separate family. Later, when Dick could walk, he and I would sneak across heavily traveled Route 111, which ran between our cottage and the farmhouse, much to the dismay of Mom and the absolute fright of Grandma Amy. Finally, Grandma Amy and Grandpa Lloyd decided to divide the farmhouse into two domiciles, and soon after that, we moved across the road.

The coming of World War II changed our lives forever, somewhat for good at the start but, ultimately, for bad. Because of his deafness, Dad was exempt from military service, and since times had become tight in the labor market, he was in demand. Apparently, too, Dad and his stepfather had had a falling out. Grandpa Lloyd, the only paternal grandfather I knew, was very much a product of that tough-minded, tightfisted family from Scotland and had little use for emotion, let alone any sympathy for a "deefie." (No matter how often I corrected him he always pronounced "deaf" as "deef.")

Mom was thrilled at the prospect of leaving the farm because she had always been a small-town and city girl and had never adjusted well to the farming life. Because she had spent most of her adolescence in the Deaf school, she had almost no practical skills whatever, and she was not a good cook. Her use of "store-bought" was a continual thorn in Grandma's side. Grandma believed store-bought food was a great extravagance and that we ought to be using the bounties the farm provided. To make matters worse, Grandma was a skilled cook, and her food, simple though it was, compares with any I have had in four-star restaurants here and abroad. Mom's particular gift was for sewing, and she used every opportunity to cut a corner on wardrobes for herself, her husband, and her kids by sewing us plenty of shirts and outfits to keep us looking decently cared for and to hide our poverty as best she could.

My socially driven, gregarious mother had been cut off for too long from close contact with Deaf culture and craved the animated, entertaining, and extended conversations she loved to carry on with her many Deaf friends. The city was to her a paradise within reach. We left Defiance in 1942 and headed for Lima, where we lived temporarily with a Deaf family, the Shimps. Lima proved, however, to be only a way station on the road to a much bigger city—Toledo.

2

Toledo (1942–1949)

IN SEPTEMBER 1942, we arrived in Toledo, two innocent parents and their two boys, unprepared for the life they were about to face. Sheltered by a rigid institutional upbringing, from the farm and from the small town, my young parents, with their sons in tow, presented themselves in all their naïveté to become citizens of the city. Of course, Toledo was not New York or Chicago, but still, it held some surprises for them, as did the war and the economic recession that followed it. The experience almost broke the back of our family and of many Deaf families who were left to fend for themselves once the war came to an end. Dad was part of President Roosevelt's civilian army because he was "unfit" for military duty and, therefore, became one of the ranks of workers who provided the arms and armor for the war effort and one of those whom America abandoned once the war was over.

Dickie and Bobby at the Shimp home, Lima, Ohio, 1942.

After a short stay in a small, furnished place on Dorr Street, we relocated to a modest second-floor apartment at 1956 Franklin Avenue, where we lived for the next seven years. Dad got work at Willys-Overland, which was humming with activity, as the plant had already geared up for the production of war materiel. Lend-Lease had put life into the automotive industry as America became the arsenal of democracy, and my father, a young man of twenty-five with a healthy body and the ability to learn skills despite his handicap, was in demand. Pearl Harbor had been attacked, and America entered the war with full force.

It is 1942, and my father operates a punch press at Willys-Overland where he is an excellent worker and wins awards for productivity. He is doing his part in the war effort, but he knows his own mind and is not ashamed of his Deafness.

He notices that the punch press he is assigned to is working errati-cally, and he almost loses a hand when it comes thumping down unexpect-edly. He complains to his foreman and is told to keep at his work, but when the press almost catches his hand again, Dad refuses to work on it and complains to his shop steward. So they move him to another machine.

Later that night (Dad was on second shift), he finds out that another worker lost three fingers to the erratic press. He says to himself, "Thank God for the union."

Our two-bedroom apartment was near the center of the city, in a block of respectable tenements erected at the turn of the century, which were just now beginning to show some blight. Later, in the '60s, the area would become part of the ghetto and then be demolished to make way for urban renewal. The last time I saw it, in the '70s, the whole block was taken up by an ugly gray warehouse-like affair.

The building was owned by Irving Miller Sr., who with his son Irving Jr., ran a small clothing store in a matching structure next door at the corner of Woodruff and Franklin. The apartment had a living room, dining room, kitchen, bath, storage room, and two bed-rooms. My parents occupied the smaller bedroom, and Dick and I, the larger one, which later had to accommodate two more boys after my brothers Art and John were born. In fact, the four of us boys shared two double beds in one room until I left for college in 1956.

Elsewhere in the city, where I do not exactly recall, my unmarried Aunt Dorothy Sowers, my Deaf aunt and my favorite, lived and worked for the Libbey Glass Company where she would remain until she retired in the '80s.

The neighborhood had that commingling of cultures, but of course, only white cultures, typical of the inner city before urban renewal and white flight. Above us for a time lived an older Canadian couple without children. When they moved back to their native Canada, they were replaced by a Catholic family whose son was a buddy of mine. Harmon Miller, our next-door neighbor and the son of our landlord, was Jewish, as were several of my school friends. Many of my other friends were Polish Catholic, one of the largest ethnic minorities in Toledo. My parents told me we were of German descent, but later, I learned that the Miller family had emigrated from Switzerland.

My family had been pretty much mainline Methodist, out of deference to my Grandma Sowers, who was a dedicated Methodist, and my Grandma Amy, who faithfully attended the Methodist church in Junction. In Toledo, Dick and I went to Ashland Avenue Baptist Church because it was within walking distance and convenient and because Mom and Dad believed in churchgoing, whatever the religion. They usually attended deaf services downtown on St. Clair Street, which were sponsored by the Lutheran church, and I also would often go. Ashland Avenue Baptist was a bit High Church, meaning the minister wore a morning suit with a swallowtail coat on Sundays, and baptisms took place in a large basin hidden behind dark velvet curtains that were drawn open when it was in use. Thank God I had already been baptized in the waters of the Auglaize River back in Defiance. I thought the whole ritual to be rather spooky. Dick, however, was not so fortunate. He received the traditional Baptist immersion at Ashland Avenue Church.

For a time right after the war, Aunt Eleanor (Mom's sister) and Uncle Bob Householder lived below us with their first daughter Sharyn, but soon, they moved away to the small town of Bloomdale where Uncle Bob began a business of his own. Their apartment was then taken by the Turners, who also had a small daughter. Emily Turner was a nice woman with lots of time on her hands, and her husband Malcolm was a quiet, almost anonymous man who, my mother told me, worked nights in an illegal gambling casino. Often, the police came to our apartment making mysterious inquiries about the Turners, but I was told to clam up, and I did.

After Aunt Dorothy married, she and her Deaf husband Warren Chaplin lived in a small apartment on Vermont Avenue just a block behind us. Dorothy was my favorite aunt, a fun-loving, gay, energetic, beautiful woman who delighted in entertaining her nephews with joking and teasing, and Uncle Warren was even more fun. He had a wry sense of humor and loved to kid us. Aunt Dorothy had no children, so she and Uncle Warren more or less adopted us kids as their own, and there were many times in my life when they were extremely generous to me. Whenever birthdays, holidays, or special events came around, I could always expect a nice gift from Aunt Dottie and Uncle Warren.

Uncle Warren and Aunt Dorothy Chaplin, my mother's Deaf sister, Toledo, Ohio, c. 1948.

Warren worked at a lithographing firm, in keeping with the tradition of Deaf people finding occupations in the printing industry.
Because Aunt Dottie and Uncle Warren were both in steady jobs
(among Deaf people, a "steady job" was a sign of having arrived)
and childless, they tended to live higher up the scale than Mom and
Dad, a circumstance that must have been a source of some friction,
although there never seemed to be any. Mom and Dad had the kids
to take care of, so they weren't always able to keep up with Dorothy
and Warren's high life.

One of the benefits of having my aunt and uncle close by was that
they communicated directly with me in ASL, not in home signing,
and a lot of the signs I came to know I learned from them because
they expected me to act like a Deaf person in their presence. I was
treated no differently from anyone else. Once in a while, I would use
these "new" signs with my parents, and they would be stunned, as
if I had penetrated some secret society they belonged to, and they
would demand to know where I learned them. I would simply
brush them off and say, "Oh, I just picked it up at the Club" (the
Toledo Silent Club, a social club of the Deaf community). Often, I
would have to ask to have things repeated, and Uncle Warren would
ream me out because I had such poor signing skills for someone who
was the son of Deaf parents. I can feel his fiery eyes on me as he signs
to me, "Shame on you (index finger pointed at me, the other index
finger sliding over it in the sign for *shame*), poor signing, mother
father deaf. Yes, you (again, the pointing finger)."

One of my places to escape to, especially when home became un-
bearable, as it did later on, was the Toledo Public Library, an art deco
building at Michigan Avenue and Adams Street, which held the most
fascinating books and had the most glorious children's library I have
ever seen. It still thrives today and is one of the jewels in the library
system's crown. In the winter, I would spend many Saturdays reading

to my heart's content in the children's library. There was always the welcoming odor of pulp paper and cheap library bindings, the trim and quiet librarians who went out of their way to be helpful, and the initial but pleasant shock I experienced in discovering that I could actually take these books home. I would head off on my own for the library, which was a long walk from our apartment, but worth it.

My parents' total library consisted of a Bible, a dictionary left over from Deaf school days, and three religious books bought under duress from a Jehovah's Witness solicitor. Mom had been an easy mark for that JW evangelist. The title of one of the religious books was *God Is My Co-Pilot*, which I have since discovered is a memoir by one Robert L. Scott, published in 1944 and later made into a movie. The other two were *The Kingdom Is at Hand* and *The Truth Shall Make You Free*, both of which had frightening tales of Hell and damnation that gave me recurring nightmares about Satan and Hell for years. Later, my grandparents Sowers gave us a six-volume collection of children's stories titled *My Book House*, which they had had in their home for many years and which I would always read from whenever we visited them. We were also faithful purchasers of the JW religious paper, *The Watchtower*, which I read over and over along with *My Weekly Reader*, which was standard issue in all the schools, and of course, the *Toledo Blade* with its unique Peach Section, a peach-colored two-page pullout section, which still exists today but in a much limited format. My parents had little interest in reading outside of looking briefly through the newspaper. Dad was a reasonably good reader, but Mom had to struggle and never did really master the skill.

I loved the public library, but I reveled in visits to the Toledo Art Museum, which was located a few blocks from our home, on Monroe Street. Every year in each grade school, the museum held a competition for promising young artists, and I always managed to win. I had inherited my father's gift for drawing and painting. So every Saturday morning, I would walk to the museum for art lessons and then spend an hour or two wandering the permanent exhibits, my favorites being the Egyptian displays and the medieval cloister.

Mom and Dad's approach to supporting their kids' activities was sporadic at best. In boom times, they lavished things right and left and bought things they couldn't possibly afford to maintain in the long run. They bought a musical instrument, but didn't give any thought to the lessons; they got their boys into the scouts, but never could find any money for the uniforms. Somehow, after a lot of pestering, Dick and I got our outfits for Cub Scouts, but I finally got rousted out of the Boy Scouts for not having a uniform after weeks of pressure from my scoutmaster, who was always threatening to phone my parents. I thought, "Yeah, sure! Just go ahead and try!" Finally I quit going.

I beg Mom and Dad to buy me a trumpet so I can learn to play a musical instrument. I want to play the piano, but getting a piano is out of the question. At last, they relent, we go to a music shop downtown, and the trumpet is purchased, "on time," as usual. Warren School offers free music lessons, so Mom signs me up, and over a few months, I learn the rudiments of trumpeting.

At home, I have trouble practicing because the neighbors complain about the noise. School comes to an end, and I locate a private teacher. But then Dad gets laid off, and the lessons have to go. The trumpet and case sit in the back of the closet. Mom and Dad refuse to pawn or sell it. I take it out occasionally, but after a while, I lose interest.

After we move back to the farm, someone finds out I can "play" a trumpet. I am asked to play "Silent Night" for the Christmas pageant at the Junction Methodist Church. I stumble through it, and everyone thinks it's lovely.

At home, I was a go-between for my parents with the incessant stream of door-to-door salesmen (the telemarketers of our day) who showed up on our steps, and I soon learned how to get rid of them. Unfortunately, Mom always had a natural curiosity for gadgets and a lust to purchase. My most successful stratagems included outright misinterpreting to my parents, and I did it with no regrets. Yet we all succumbed to one of my parents' most expensive purchases. It was one I could not resist: an elegant set of the *Encyclopedia Britannica Jr.*, as it was called. It was a dumbed-down, shortened version of the Real Thing and was fantastically overpriced. I read those volumes from cover to cover and doubtless benefited from them, but I can't forget what my parents went through trying to meet the monthly payments. After I got married, they passed the set on to me, and the books lay stacked in our attic for a long time. Our daughters used to page through them as curiosities of some earlier geological age. Only once in a while did they find something they could use. Even *Britannica Jr.* got behind the times.

Some of the sinful joys of being the child of Deaf parents is that you have almost unlimited freedom in what you can do, you develop all kinds of subterfuges for getting around your parents, and you take shameless advantage of their deafness. So Dick and I had almost free reign over our time and our destinations, for good or bad. We were generally out of control. When we weren't roaming the neighborhood at will, we were down at Bellman's Market at the corner of Adams and Franklin stealing packets of Red Hots, the still popular cinnamon candy—stolen, I guess, for the thrill of it because

I hated Red Hots. Mom was busy with her friends or taking advantage of opportunities to shop and to enjoy the good money coming in, and of course, Dad was busy working for every dollar he could get.

I have been watching guys play ping-pong at the downtown Y, keeping my eye out for stray paddles because each one is worth a 25-cent deposit if you can con the desk clerk into believing you checked it out. It's a tricky business because the attendants are always on the lookout for "street urchins" trying to pull a fast one on them.

I've been coming to the Y for about a month as part of an inner-city program for kids, and I really like it. I get to swim in the pool for free. All the men and boys swim in the skinny, and the first time in the pool, it is a shock to me to find out that men have pubic hair. Tufts of dark hair shadowing limp, shriveled penises.

Everyone has left the room, and on a chair near one of the tables, I see a paddle. I pick it up casually and look to see if I've been detected. I haven't. Just as casually, I walk to the counter and slide it over to the clerk and wait for my quarter. I need that quarter to get home because I'm broke, and if I walk all the way, I'm sure to be late, and I know I'll catch hell if I am.

The clerk gives me the fish eye, "This your paddle?"

"Yup."

"You sure? I don't see any checkout stub here in the drawer." I hadn't thought of that. But I recover.

"Yeah, there was a stub. The other guy put it in the drawer. It was yellow." I'd seen the stub color for the day when I came in, so I knew I was right.

"Yeah?" Pause. "Well, okay, I guess." He knows I am lying, but he also knows I won't crack.

I pick up the quarter, spend a nickel on bus fare and another on an ice-cream cone—and still get home on time. And I still have 15 cents. I am rich.

Often, Dick and I were latch-keyed so my parents could get away to the Deaf Club. Left unsupervised, we often got into terrible scrapes. One afternoon, we flooded the bathroom when we were filling the tub to "go swimming." Water poured into the apartment below, and once again, my parents were threatened with eviction. We were absolute hellions. Either my parents were unable to afford good sitters or the sitters they did hire refused to come back.

I always sensed a great cultural divide between my parents and their larger Hearing families when it came to expressing personal feelings because, in our immediate family, we tended to behave emotionally, to have real rockem-sockem arguments, and to put our feelings up front. My parents acted that way toward each other, and I suppose anyone who might have chanced to witness some of their set-tos would

Arthur and Ora Sowers, my mother's parents, 1953.

have assumed they had a very shaky marriage. Even my father, who was a man of great patience and tact, could put on a real show. It is true that there were rocky times in the marriage, but truer it is that this was the way I was brought up, and it is the way I still tend to behave, and it has been a real struggle for me, particularly in the halls of Academia, to restrain my naturally emotional behavior. On the other hand, my wife is a model of discretion and control, and over the years, we have often had to come to terms with that cultural divide between us.

At some point, as my kids were growing up, one of them commented to me, "Boy, Grandma and Grandpa sure do fight a lot!" It had not occurred to me that they would have a completely different perspective on my parents' behavior than I did. I am not a behavioral specialist, but it doesn't take a rocket scientist to recognize the causes: a language, ASL, that depends heavily on body and facial gestures that can often be interpreted by outsiders as "emotional behavior"; a clannish, strong sense of social identity that functions both as a means of bonding and as a protection from the prejudice or the often misguided, often destructive do-goodism of the Hearing; a childhood and adolescence frequently deprived and an education that was language-delayed and deprived; and a powerful sense of individual worth, which is a quality almost all Deaf people exhibit. These factors naturally lead to behavior that the Hearing world often regards as socially unacceptable but that the Deaf community recognizes as essential to survival.

In the fourth grade, I have my first real encounter with death. My close friend Robert Gold, who lives on 10th Avenue, is hit by a truck on his way home from school.

As I come in the door, I tell my mother, in a frenzy of excitement, not realizing how grave this moment is, "Mom, Mom, Robert Gold got hit by a truck and got killed!" Immediately, Mom is overcome and begins crying, and I can't really fathom why. She has seen him only a couple of times when I brought him over to play, but she remembers.

Mom and Dad take me to the funeral home, visit (through me) with Robert's mother, and see to it that I am not sheltered from this moment. I resolve to keep forever in my mind the image of his trim little body, suited, his blonde hair in a neat brush cut, and his angelic face.

Even though I'm too old to be picked up, Dad carries me out of the funeral home to the car. I press my face into his neck and begin to cry.

As a participant in a Deaf family, I followed the lead of my parents, but in the Hearing world, I dreaded moments when their guard would come down and they would "act out" in public, which hardly ever occurred because they recognized that there was one form of behavior for the Deaf world and another for the Hearing.

In 1944, ready for the first grade (children did not attend Kindergarten then), I was sent off down the street to Warren School at the corner of Woodruff and Warren, where I proved to be a bright student, but painfully shy. What made matters worse, I was deathly afraid my mother would be called in and I would have to interpret for her as she and my teacher discussed my "problem." My parents were in the middle of their divorce (which I discuss later), so Mom was on her own with this responsibility.

I had already learned to read and had kept it a secret, but Grandma Amy caught me out one day and was astonished. The news that there was a "genius" in their midst put the parents and grandparents into a state of excitement. In school, I got to bypass the boring Dick and Jane readers that were a part of every kid's reading education because I was already beyond them. I was excused from reading class and given other books to work with. Of course, I was not a genius, just a bright kid, as I would eventually discover. To my grandparents, the news was a contradiction of all they had believed about Deaf people while, to my mother, it was a salvation. She may have been "deaf and dumb," but by God she had given birth to a bright kid! From then on, I was treated as a prodigy and, eventually, became a curse to my brothers, who had to follow me through the grades, harangued by parents and teachers alike about the accomplishments of their big brother.

I am sitting with Mom in the principal's office at Warren School in Toledo, and the principal, Miss Bishop, and my third-grade teacher, Mrs. Coady, look at us both as if we have committed some terrible offense. It is fall, and the room is slightly steamy, and the heating pipes clank ominously. Mom is beautifully dressed, in hose and high heels, and elaborately made up, in the fashion of the time, which is the year 1946. She looks like a pregnant Rita Hayworth. She is carrying my brother John, who will be born in January, and she is not feeling well.

Finally Miss Bishop speaks. "Bobby, tell your mother that we are very happy with your school work, but we feel you are too shy and withdrawn. Tell her we are concerned that you are not relating to the other students as we'd like. We think you need more contact with regular people." I want to stand up and say, "That's because I am shy, not because my folks are deaf. I'm SHY! And my folks ARE REGULAR PEOPLE!" But, of course, I'm too shy to say so.

I struggle to speak. "What is 'relate'?" I ask. She explains. I turn to Mom and try to tell her what Miss Bishop has said but omit the part

about "regular people." She signs to me, "Tell her you are a good boy,
but you have always been shy, and you have been through a hard time
at home. Tell her your dad and I have hard times now."

I brace. Mom and I continue our private dialogue. I say to her, "I
don't want to tell Miss Bishop about home. I don't want to tell her. It's
none of her business."

She answers, "Don't argue, just tell her what I said. Tell her things are
hard at home, you are a smart boy and a good boy, and you will do better."

I tell Miss Bishop but omit the part about my home life, while Mrs.
Coady looks on, suspiciously, certain that I'm pulling a fast one on them.
Then I realize Mom has been watching my lips and knows I have not
told all. Miss Bishop nods, they both display smiles that look more like
grimaces, and the session blessedly comes to an end. I wonder to myself
what they must make of this little boy who has to explain himself to
them by interpreting his mother's conversation.

Back home, Mom threatens to give me a spanking for lying to her.
Then she looks at me, lovingly, and tells me to go out and play.

The cadre of professional educators who place such a high value on
"socialization" has always put me off. As a child of Deaf parents, I
always felt that I would forever be an "other," a member of a marked
minority, and that it was incredibly naïve of me or my teachers to
think that I would ever "fit in." I was not the problem; my teachers
were the problem. If not my identity as a CODA, then my intense
shyness would always mark me in some way as being a kid apart,
and I had a right to be treated honestly by a world that had set my
parents apart. The hypocrisy of their attitude was too obvious to me.

But in many other ways, I was an ordinary kid. I played Germans
and Japs, Cops and Robbers, Cowboys and Indians. On the radio,

I listened to the *Lone Ranger*, the *Green Hornet*, the *Shadow*. I read *Superman*, *Batman*, and *Captain Marvel*. And I lusted after my buddy Jimmy Stone's mother in ways that were only a pale manifestation of the stirrings that would overtake me in a few years.

Even though I was a shy and retiring kid, I could also be a surprisingly devilish kid. I had the freedom to indulge my bad behavior because I was always thought to be a "nice boy." But I had developed a kind of low cunning, so often I deflected blame onto my brother Dick, who was beginning to develop a reputation as a problem child. Just a few months ago, my mother remarked to me that I was such a "nice boy" as a child, which startled me because I had assumed she would have eventually seen through my "nice boy" facade. I know that, later, my two younger brothers gave my parents fits, but I knew it only by hearsay because, by that time, I'd gone off to the university and was on my own.

I'm about five, and it's midafternoon. Mom has been busily arranging clothes on the wooden dryers she unfolds every washday, and I'm looking forward to playing "hideout" with my brother. Amid the steamy sheets and shirts, we make secret lairs for ourselves, and squirrel away toys and treats. Mom is occupied with the wringer washer, which requires constant attention, so I make my own snack.

As I pour milk from the bottle, it slips from my hand and crashes to the floor, and breaks into jagged pieces. Milk is everywhere. Mom begins to cry and shriek at me, starts chasing me around the kitchen table, but quickly, I dart through the bathroom door, dash out the connecting bedroom door, and bolt for the closet. I grab the closet door, which because of some builder's error has an inside lock, pull the door shut, and lock it.

I can hear Mom on the other side of the door, shaking and banging the door, screaming at me in that keening, piercing tocsin of a voice, as I sit huddled in the dark, thinking to myself, "What have I done? What have I done?" Near her, I can hear Dick crying.

So I start screaming back. "Go away, you mean old mom. I hate you, I hate you!"

Suddenly I realize, "What am I doing? She can't hear me, what am I doing?" So I feel for a coat, pull it off the hanger, and curl up and go to sleep.

A few hours later, my dad comes home from the factory. I hear the door rattling, then the soft guttural of my father's voice, pleading, "Bobby, open the door."

As soon as I hear Dad's voice, I know I am safe, and I turn the toggle on the lock. The door swings open, and I make a dive for Dad's legs and hold on for all I'm worth. Mom stands directly behind him, looking distraught and frustrated. I start sobbing with a passion, and Dad holds me.

Mom looks at me, then walks away.

My parents were in a constant battle with Mr. Miller, our landlord, over our loudness, our rambunctious behavior. We came close to eviction a few times, just because my parents had no idea how noisy we were. I have to confess that Mr. Miller was a very understanding and compassionate man. Finally, my father instituted "THE BELT," as we called it (always in caps), which brought us round pretty sharply, but in truth, I can't remember more than one licking I got with it. Dad's heart just wasn't in it. Among our friends, we were considered brave lads who were able to endure THE BELT. In a perverse way, corporal punishment in those days seemed to confer a medal of honor on the kids who suffered through it, and it seemed to prove that our parents really cared for us, for example, "This hurts me more than it does you." By the same token, parents who did not meet this stern obligation were often judged to be derelict in their duty. Later, when we moved back to the farm, my father was a model of humane parenting when compared to other rural fathers. Friends of mine on the farm talked about their slugging matches with "my Old Man," but Dad never put a hand on me from the age of twelve on. My mother, however, kept at it until, one day, I grabbed her wrists and held them, and began laughing. At first, she was totally stunned, but then she began laughing, too, and that episode ended corporal punishment in the Miller family, at least for me.

My own experience tells me that children of Deaf parents are inclined to mischief and love to act up. We did, and our friends who were also CODAs did, too. Gatherings of the Deaf community usually consisted of parents gesticulating intensely in ASL while their kids ran amok. We were no exception.

The Harold Winney kids, CODAs like us, were great fun, but special demons. We used to beg to go to their house. The oldest girl, Maureen, who was supposed to keep control of us when we got together, used to get into serious tussles with her brother Warren. Mr. Winney was a scarifying but kind man who had one short leg and had to wear a special shoe with a metal lift of about six inches, and his wife was a single amputee whose arm had been severed above the elbow. She signed with one hand and her remaining limb in an elegant way though, and she was a wonderful lady, and their kids were loads of fun.

My parents' social life revolved around a locale on Adams Street (now demolished) called the Toledo Silent Club, which provided a place where you could have a drink or a beer and hang out. Because it depended on a membership who had very limited financial resources, it was a seedy, rundown affair. If it hadn't been for the release it gave both my parents and their kids, we'd have never set foot in it. The organization still exists in a new location farther west on Adams Street and is called the Toledo Deaf Club, as "silent" has become a taboo word within the Deaf community. Anyone familiar with Deaf people will tell you that they are anything but silent.

The club was located on the second floor, and you arrived there by ascending a long flight of stairs from a street door. Inside, two capacious rooms were separated by a large, sliding warehouse door, counterweighted to make it easier to open. The first room had a bar at one end and some tables, and it stank wonderfully of cigarette and cigar smoke and stale beer. The walls were adorned with impressive realistic murals of scenes from the Italian theater of World War II, which were destroyed later when the building was demolished. I thought they were stirring portrayals. One mural in particular showed the liberation of Rome, with a tank coming down a Roman street, framed by some famous classical building, I think the Pantheon, in the background. The second room was a hall with a makeshift stage at one end and a couple of pool tables at the other.

The place didn't offer much for kids to do because it was mainly a gathering place for Deaf people to converse, so Dick and I spent most of our time trying to wheedle nickels and dimes from Mom and Dad for candy bars and soft drinks. At other times, when other kids would show up, we would dissolve into one screaming, racing ball of humanity. Whenever my parents got lonely, which was often, they packed us up and headed for the Silent Club, or the Club as we called it, because it was only about six or seven blocks away from our apartment. Frequently, the Club put on dramatic shows, which I loved even though, because my signing was limited, I had no idea what they were about. I distinctly recall one in particular that was performed in blackface and seemed to be some kind of minstrel show.

My father enjoyed the Club. My mother was obsessed with being there. Dad's connection with the club was athletic as well as social. He was a good basketball player and played guard on the club team, and he was a superlative fast-pitch softball pitcher. We went to the games and cheered him on. For the Toledo Silents (the name of both the softball and basketball teams), beating Hearing teams was particularly consoling because it showed them what a Deaf team could do. Dad was also a champion bowler and was the anchor of his team, which bowled at Hagerty's, a multifloor facility in downtown Toledo. Whenever Dad bowled, Mom, Dick, and I tagged along—Mom for the socializing with wives and friends of bowlers and Dick and I to cadge candy bars and pops as well as raise hell with the other CODAs.

Athletic activity was for Dad an important point of association with the Hearing community. In his excellent memoir, *My Sense of Silence*, Lennard Davis describes how his father also found contact with the Hearing community in his power-walking activities. For Dad, later in life, his bowling is what made him something of a star and a "regular guy" among his Hearing friends.

Mom craved social contact, and even when we were not at the Club, we were constantly being dragged off to a social event or whatever at one Deaf home after another. Even in the throes of childhood illness, I was bundled off to parties or get-togethers and dumped in someone's bedroom. As a child, I suffered from frequent colds and from ear infections that were very painful. Neither my mom nor my dad was one to let illnesses get in the way of good times, until finally at one party, I suffered a ruptured eardrum and had to be taken home and then to the doctor's in the morning.

On other occasions, my parents could be as dedicated to their kids as any parents could be. Sometime in the winter of 1943–44,

my brother Dick came down with pneumonia, and the family shift-
ed to crisis alert because the only viable treatment at the time was
the administration of sulfa. Penicillin was available but only in very
limited quantities until after the war, and so pneumonia, especially
in a young child (Dick was about three going on four at the time),
was considered a life-threatening disease. My parents marshaled every
bit of their parenting skills, neighbors assisted around the clock, and
the doctor stopped in every several hours to see how my little brother was faring. Finally, very early in the morning of our watch, Mom
woke me up and asked whether I wanted to see my brother. I was
so glad to see him, the little pale, blonde boy just barely able to say
Hi to me. His fever had broken. Mom, Dad, I, as well as friends and
neighbors both Deaf and Hearing, were thrilled to see young Dickie
get better and better as the days passed.

To get us two boys out of the house, my mother would send us off
to Saturday movies at the Loop or the Royal theaters in the heart of
downtown, which could be reached by streetcar or bus. Every Saturday, Dick and I set out for the most recent double feature, usually
a double billing of cowboy movies, and stayed all afternoon because,
in those days, you were allowed to stay and watch the two movies for
as long as you liked, and we never found just one viewing satisfying.
Usually, we would take our return bus fare and buy goodies with it,
and then walk all the way home from downtown. We also followed
the common practice of the day of entering in the middle of a film
and watching it through to the end, watching the second film, and
then watching the first film through from beginning to end. As a
student of narrative, I've marveled at how similar this practice must
have been to the bardic custom of reciting parts of sagas.

As the children of Deaf parents, we were constantly being taken off
to see movies. My mother was a great fan of horror movies and was
constantly hauling us off to Frankenstein and Dracula and Wolfman

movies, which frightened me out of my wits, so much so that I was in college before I could even watch a horror movie without having nightmares. No expense was spared to catch the latest films. Those were the days of the great movie theaters, and a high moment in my moviegoing life was when Aunt Dottie and Uncle Warren took me and my parents to see a rerun of *Gone with the Wind* after the war at the sumptuous Loewe's Valentine on St. Clair Street.

Even though we couldn't afford it, we bought the first television set in the neighborhood and watched literally everything—wrestling, the Gillette Friday Night Fights, baseball games, and my favorite, *Kukla, Fran, and Ollie*, a kids' puppet show that was very popular in the early days of television. When programming was off, we watched the test pattern, and my dad spent untold hours fine-tuning our little Emerson set. The major tuning controls were in the back of the set, so he would have to prop a large mirror in front of the set to see the screen as he made his complicated adjustments.

My job as TV watcher, of course, was to interpret the audio portion of the programs for my parents, which I enjoyed doing, and to this day, I think it helped me develop my skill at writing plot summaries. I was always amazed at how quickly my parents could size up the plot of a story on TV once I laid out the identities and relationships of the characters and the main story line. Closed captioning has brought much of this interpreting activity to an end, and I miss it because it was a bonding experience for me and my parents. In a freakish way, being able to interpret gave me a kind of power over my parents, which I secretly enjoyed. To this day, I am an avid TV watcher, to the embarrassment of my wife and kids.

Vacations were unheard of in my family, but trips back to Defiance on weekends and holidays were special treats because Dick and I got to romp in the barns and fields and eat Grandma Amy's luscious cooking. We also got to sleep in the upstairs bedroom, a large attic-type room with two double beds, both of which were scrumptiously comfortable and bouncy. Another family now occupied our old digs next door.

My parents really didn't care to visit the farm, and had it not been such fun for Dick and me, I don't think they'd have bothered to go. It was farther away than Fostoria, and that meant an overnight stay. Besides, Grandma Amy had no signing skills whatever, which made conversation especially difficult. Their favorite trips were always to Fostoria where they could visit back and forth with my Aunt Dottie and Uncle Warren as well as with Mom's mother and other sisters Eleanor and Jean, both of whom had a little command of ASL and a genuine love of and desire to relate to their Deaf sisters.

Trips to Fostoria were less appealing to me, especially as I got older, unless our cousin Sharyn Householder happened to be visiting too, and then we would go over to the Fostoria pool and swim, or just roam around the neighborhood. Most of the time, I sat in the tiny sun room of that tiny house and read those volumes of *My Book House* by Olive Beaupré Miller and a little paperback collection about the Lost Battalion of World War I, which I had read so many times I had practically memorized it.

3

Summer Idylls (1943–1948)

*I*t is July 1943, one month before my accident. I am almost five. *Grandpa Lloyd and I are fishing from the end of the dock on the river at the Other Place. He is sitting on a five-gallon tar bucket and I on an upturned old pail, a miniature image of him. The sun shines brightly, but the air is cool and damp in the early morning hour, and we are content knowing we have a nice stringer of bullheads and cat-fish to carry back to the house. And I am looking forward to a special treat—a plump, tart apple from the tree along the lane we walked down to the river.*

Things have been a little slow for the last half hour, so Grandpa recites his special mantra for getting fish to bite:

"Fishie, fishie, in the brook,
Come and bite my little hook,
You'll be the captain and I'll be the cook!"

Suddenly, the tip of my old cane pole dips to the water, and the line starts cutting crazy circles in the surface. Grandpa hoots, "Bobby, Bobby, you got a big one! Bring 'im in, quick."

But the fish is more than I can handle. "Grandpa, help me, help me! I can't, I can't!"

He reaches over and grasps the lower end of the pole and levers the fish up, while I hold on. It is a sheephead (freshwater drum) of about three pounds. I am so thrilled, I almost cry. Everything seems wonderful.

For several summers during this Toledo period, I stayed with my Grandpa and Grandma Newton at the Other Place, their little farm in Paulding County that they retired to during the summer months. At the time, it was an arrangement that seemed to benefit everyone, but ultimately, it did me more harm than good because it separated me from my parents and caused the breach between us to widen. Every August, when I came back to Toledo, I had to go through a wrenching period of adjustment, when my parents and I would fight bitterly, until I was finally integrated back into the family once again and could take up my responsibilities to and for my parents.

But I loved the country and liked being with my grandparents. The Other Place was thirty-eight acres, half pasture and half arable land, in an idyllic setting a few miles southwest of the home farm. Like the home farm, it was also on the banks of the Auglaize River, off the Anthony Wayne Trace, the route General Wayne followed in the summer of 1794 to reach Fort Defiance. The farmhouse stood at the end of a lane, with a huge elm tree in front and a barn, chicken coop, woodshed, outhouse, and granary scattered around it. On one side of the house was a large garden that was raided regularly by a woodchuck, or groundhog, that lived under the house. But the plot grew enough for the three of us humans and the groundhog as well as the rabbits that showed up in the early mornings while the dew was on.

From the home farm, Grandpa brought along one cow, Eleanor, so we had plenty of milk and cream. Grandma kept a small flock of laying hens, and I raised broilers (frying chickens), which I sold for spending money.

At the Other Place, Grandpa had his own bedroom downstairs off the front room, and Grandma and I slept in two big double beds on the second floor, under the eaves.

It is a warm July night. I am lying in bed upstairs at the Other Place, tossing and turning, running wildly through tongues of flame. I am pursued by devils that threaten to catch me and tear me limb from limb. I look back at them as I keep running. I look ahead and see the Prince of Darkness himself blocking my path. He is demonic, oddly lascivious in his red and blue attire, like Superman gone bad. I scream at him, and then someone has hold of my arm and is shaking me.

"Bobby, Bobby, wake up for goodness sake!" It is Grandma.

I cry, "Oh, Grandma, I had a devil dream. Can I sleep in your bed?"

"Well, sure, you come on over here."

I crawl in beside her under the thin quilt. Everything is perfect.

Every morning Grandpa would get up and milk Eleanor by hand, then have a hearty farm breakfast of jowl bacon, eggs, potatoes, toast, pie, and coffee, and then take me fishing. The milk we didn't drink was run through a separator and the cream sold in town, except for a part of it that Grandma churned into delicious butter. The skim was left to clabber and then was fed to the chickens, or sometimes Grandma made Schmierkäse, or cottage cheese, which she called simply "smearcase," one of the few German words left in the family vocabulary from its Swiss heritage. Yogurt was an unknown product then, and we never would have eaten it anyway because it would have been "fitten only for the hogs." My grandparents also banned any kind of pasta, except for Spätzel or noodles, and they very definitely banned garlic, the Italian Curse. But my parents, having eaten both foods at the state school, shoveled tons of both down us kids. No matter how much I begged Grandma to cook spaghetti, she refused, and Grandpa referred to it as "fish worms."

At first, the summer farm had no electricity and never did have any plumbing or running water, but electricity came soon after I began to spend my summers there. Water for washing was taken from an old barrel that collected rainwater from the roof and, later, from a brick-lined cistern at the end of the porch. Our drinking water came from a well. An outhouse stood at the end of a short path, just in front of the chicken coop. The door was forever swinging open at inopportune moments because the inside latch was missing, and consequently, its inner décor often was revealed to an unsuspecting audience of anyone who happened to be around, in, or near the cottage. Ladies would carefully pull the door closed and hope it would stay closed, but it never did. The door would slowly creak open, just out of their reach, and there they would sit, plump Ohio farm wives with their dresses up around their pale thighs and their drawers down around their ankles, with me gawking at them. They would gasp and clumsily pull the door shut, but it would always swing open again, and I would still be standing there, frozen in place, eyes bugged out like Barney Fife's. I should have had manners enough to get the hell out, but every time it happened, I was too scared to move.

Chained to a large tree not too far from the outhouse was Grandpa's rabbit dog Sport, a smallish redbone-type hound of nondescript origin and no talent whatever, who from time to time would raise hell by breaking his chain and running wild among the chickens. Once in a while, to prove he was a menace, he'd manage to catch a couple. If he did, they were goners, and Grandma would once again have another reason, actually two, to get rid of him. I never could play with him because he was so wild he'd knock me down and jump all over me. He was never taken hunting because he would always run off, and then Grandpa would have to spend the rest of the day trying to track him down. Obedience was not a word in his canine lexicon. Sport's demise remains a mystery to me, but one summer I came out to the Other Place to find that Sport had been replaced by Brownie, who had some beagle in him but otherwise was just as crazy as Sport was.

Mostly I passed the summer days listening to ball games on the radio, rooting for the White Sox, the Tigers, and the popular local team, the Cleveland Indians. My last summer at the Other Place was memorable because that was the year the Indians won the pennant, and all summer long, I followed the achievements of Lou Boudreau, the player-manager, and his stars, Bob Feller, Bob Lemon, Gene Bearden, Satchel Paige, Jim Hegan, Dale Mitchell, Joe Gordon, Ken Keltner, and the great Larry Doby.

Almost every morning, I would go fishing with Grandpa Lloyd for sheephead and catfish in the Auglaize River, which ran behind the farm at the back of a field. Most of the afternoons I spent playing with my cousin Everett Miller, who was a year older than I and lived on the adjacent farm to the south. Everett's dad Ralph, Dad's first cousin and the son of Uncle Will and Aunt Edna, farmed the Other Place. Directly across the road were the Weaver girls, who became surrogate parents to me, watched over me, taught me to ride a bike, and teased me without end.

Every Saturday morning early after breakfast and the milking, my grandparents and I would head for Defiance to do the weekly shopping and to sell our cream and a few eggs. Grandma shopped at the A&P, Grandpa went to Hoyt's Hardware, and I was allowed to walk up and down Clinton Street at my pleasure. I got 25 cents allowance and usually spent 20 cents on a gadget or toy and a nickel on a cherry Coke at Rosenberger's Drug Store. On the way home, we would stop at the home farm where Grandma and Grandpa would see to their living quarters and Grandma would do a little light cleaning. Then they would sit down with the hired man, as he was referred to, and "settle up," which meant that, first, the accounts, which Grandma kept, would be gone over, and then Grandpa and the hired man would go over the work to be done for the week. This business arrangement gave the impression to folks round about that my grandparents were rich, which was far from true, although they had substantial savings, probably upwards of $10,000, which was considerable for the time. But they accumulated that money by cautious hoarding and even more cautious spending. By 1945, my grandparents had begun to draw Social Security, which, together with the farm profits, allowed them a modest income.

Early one afternoon, Grandpa, Grandma, and I have stopped at the farm to do the settling up. Bill Meeks, the hired man, gets into a shout-

ing match with Grandpa, and Grandpa yells, "Goddammit, Bill, you
will not have those cows tested!"

Meeks answers, "Lloyd, you got to do it. You can't sell milk knowing
what we know!"

Meeks believes the herd is infected with "bangs," or brucellosis, a
bovine disease that causes cows to abort their calves. I learn later, in the
winter, that Meeks had the cows tested on his own, and they tested neg-
ative, so the herd was saved. But Grandpa is so angered by what he did
that he fires him or, at least, they part company.

Depending on Grandpa's mood and how things were going on
the farm, these sessions with the hired man could be tense. Usually,
I tried to sneak away and wander around among the buildings or
play with the hired man's kids, if they weren't busy with their chores.
Grandpa's general approach to all problems was to avoid any kind
of expense at all costs. He had no real sense of spending money to
make money. In his economic calculus, you made money by not
spending it and by hoarding it, so around the farm, the hired men
constantly had to make do. They went without essential tools or else
bought them themselves. They had to work with machinery that broke
down constantly and had to be repaired—usually at the cheapest
cost—or with machinery that hovered on the verge of breakdown
and was literally held together by baling wire.

After business was taken care of, we drove on the few miles to the
old Miller homestead where Aunt Edna and Uncle Will lived and
visited with them for a while. And then it was back home where we
unloaded groceries and settled in for another week. If we had to
make an emergency purchase, we could always drive over to Charloe

or to Junction, both of which had small grocery stores and were only
a few miles away.

*It is August 1943, and I have just turned five. My idyllic life is, in
the words of Yeats, about to be "changed, utterly."*

*Grandma and Grandpa are doing chores. I am alone in the kitchen
and decide to open a Coke, which I have been saving in the icebox that
sits on the back porch. I spy the opener hanging on a nail on the side of
a cabinet. A yardstick hangs directly underneath it on the same nail. So
I decide to use the yardstick to flip the opener off the nail. The can opener
has a sharp, pointed end for puncturing and slicing open can lids. When
I flip it off the nail, it drops straight into my open right eye, penetrates the
cornea, and punctures the lens. Everything becomes cloudy, then deep
red. I scream "Grandma, Grandma!" and she comes running from the
granary, and Grandpa is not far behind. They rush me to Dr. Mouser's
office in Paulding where the eye is treated.*

*The next day, my parents drive down from Toledo and take me
home, and then begins a long series of visits to an ophthalmologist and
an interminable series of eye drops, packs, and exams.*

I lost the sight in the eye, but thanks to the unflagging care of
my mother and the skill of the ophthalmologist who was recom-
mended by our downstairs neighbors the Turners, physically, my eye
was saved. Early photos of me at about that age are easy to identify
as either pre- or post-loss because I developed a noticeable case of
strabismus when my right eye became inactive, and I was required
to wear eyeglasses, which I hated, more to protect my left eye than

to correct my vision. Those were the days of glass lenses, and I was forever breaking them and causing another major money crisis for my mom and dad. To this day, I find it painful to look at photos of me that reveal my cross-eye, and as a kid, I abandoned my eyeglasses whenever I could get away with it, even though the glasses masked slightly the cast of my eye. Over the years, I'd suffered the usual taunts about my glasses and the weird-looking eye and gradually came to accommodate myself to my fate—a one-eyed, physically inept kid with Deaf parents. Only a few years ago, in reading the fiction writer Jim Harrison's confessions about the grievous psychic damage he suffered when he lost his eye did I realize how deeply I had been affected.

Grandma must have seen the event as a judgment for all the times she had doubted Mom's ability to care for her children. One day, out of the blue, she said to me in a confessional tone, "Oh, Bobby, you don't know how much I hated it when you lost your eye. I sure hated that. I'd have given both my eyes to keep it from happening." Later, when I was in high school and showing definite talent, my grandparents committed themselves to sending me to college, and I believe in some way it was payback for the guilt they both felt over the loss of my eye.

More serious was my loss of depth perception, which depends on binocular vision. I was just developing my athletic skills, and the effect of that loss was to throw me into a regression as I also began to lose eye-limb coordination. All I could hope was that, over time, I would develop compensations, which I have done, but I never did develop the ability to play baseball well, the game I love. Recently, during a visit to the Louisville Slugger Museum here in my home city, I stood in a simulated batting box and watched a pitch thrown at ninety miles per hour. Fuhgeddaboudit. I hadn't a clue. From that day in August 1943 forward, I had to steel myself to stand up to a pitch or field a ball.

Those summers became idylls of rural comfort, and I was the totally spoiled kid who had nothing to do but play all day, perform a few chores, go fishing, ride my bike, and generally be the center of attention of doting grandparents who, in spite of their lack of personal warmth, indulged me in ways my parents would have found shocking. Yet, if I take a hard look at those summer interludes, I can remember many times when, as I got older, I yearned to be home with my parents and Dick as well as with my city pals, doing all kinds of interesting city things, even pilfering at Bellman's Market.

Occasionally, my parents would come down from Toledo to visit on weekends, and I looked forward to their arrival. I would hug and kiss them and make over them, and they did the same with me. My grandparents were wonderful to me, but they weren't Mom and Dad. During those visits, I'd take Dick off on jaunts around the little farm to show him what was what.

One summer, several weeks before I was to return to Toledo, some friends of my grandparents showed up unexpectedly for a weekend stay. These sort of social intrusions, which would never be tolerated today, especially by city dwellers, were the common mode in the country. As the friends were getting ready to drive back to Toledo, I suggested that maybe I could ride with them and save Mom and Dad a trip down. The Andersons were quick to be willing to oblige, but Grandma stepped in and, in her own subtle way, quashed the plan. I was totally wiped out at the prospect of two or three more weeks of separation, and I snuck off to the barn where I sobbed away, something I could always do openly at home because my parents usually weren't aware of my crying, and if I did carry on, they just took it as natural behavior and ignored it. My grandparents, on the other hand, saw any extreme expression of emotion as a moral failing. "Don't cry. Be a man." Now that I think of it, I don't believe I ever heard my father say that to me.

After 1948, the summer visits ended, to the disappointment of my grandparents and, I think, somewhat of my parents, too, who found life a little more manageable with one of their kids out of the way for the summer. I picked up with my friends in the city and went back to my old habits of petty thievery, long games of back-yard softball, trips to the library and to the movies, and visits to the Deaf Club.

4   Hard Times (1944–1949)

*L*ate at night, Dick and I are playing in our bedroom under tented bedcovers. We know our parents can't hear what we are doing. There are just the two of us—no younger brothers to bother us yet. Suddenly, from the kitchen, we hear someone pound on the table and then the deep guttural of Dad's voice and the high shriek of my mother's, and I know something is wrong because my parents never vocalize to each other unless they are really angry.

We creep out into the dark dining room and peer into the lighted kitchen where an eerie pantomime is taking place between our parents. They are arguing at full tilt, their hands flying menacingly within inches of each other, threatening at any moment to become weapons. My mother is weeping uncontrollably.

Dick says, "What they doing?"

I console him, "Don't worry. They're just having a little fight."

"They fighting? Do they got guns?" he asks, wide-eyed. As World War II kids, we expect all fights to involve guns.

I answer, "Yeah, they're fighting, but it's not big, so they don't have guns. Let's go back to bed."

As we turn to enter the bedroom I glance over my shoulder toward the kitchen and think I see my parents looking at us woefully. But no one comes. We are alone.

In 1944, a few years after our move to Toledo, the seemingly idyllic marriage of Richard and Elizabeth Miller came apart. Even during the peaceful times, my parents were daily wrapped in one argument or another, but now they took the conflicts to another level, to animated, emotional, violent confrontations at the kitchen table. My way of coping was to grab Dick and beat it for the dining room. We would both hunker down in the dark room behind the doorframe and watch the frantic signing between them, and I would translate as much as I could make out, which was not much, and even those bits and pieces have faded into mystery with the passing of time. Now, almost sixty years after the fact, the causes of this breach between my parents are well kept secrets, locked up with them or buried with those who have passed on. I've agonized over that dark drama a great deal but can only guess at its causes.

As a five-year-old going on six, I was hardly able to fathom the complications of my parents' marital life, let alone comprehend it in that inaccessible language, the adult idiom of ASL, which my parents kept closed to me. Their unthinking habit of "acting out," unconcerned about the effect on us kids, didn't do us any good. I don't think they quite grasped how prescient I was. At least, they did not seem to be concerned about it. As I grew older and savvier, they became even more cautious with their conversation. In Hearing families, parents make special efforts not to be overheard. ("Shh! The children are listening!") In Deaf families, signing is impossible to carry on sotto voce, although Deaf people consider it extreme bad manners to horn in on a conversation by staring at the signers. Anyone who approaches Deaf people in conversation always has the obligation to get himself or herself acknowledged by the conversers, usually by a simple exchange of glances.

Episodes of conflict continued day after day, and Dick and I adjusted to the confusion. I was preparing to enter the first grade at Warren School and very much looked forward to it. Whatever shyness I showed in my behavior was now exacerbated by a steady withdrawal into my own and my brother's world where I could feel safe from what I considered the threatening world of adult violence. Although I never witnessed any overt acts of violence, only threats, those constant threats, the heightened sense of emotional conflict that I think communicates more readily in the total body language of ASL than in spoken English, served to keep me in a constant state of fear. After all the exposure to make-believe violence I'd had as a "war child," I now understood the difference between real and make-believe because I'd seen real threatened violence naked and up close. At one point, I couldn't speak for a day, and the nightmares came regularly for weeks after.

Not long after, Mom and Dad decided to file for divorce. I was always a daddy's boy, and the loss of my father was something I struggled with. Mom and Dad separated, and their divorce was finalized on November 3, 1944. The grounds were conveniently given as "gross neglect of duty." Mom got the kids and furniture plus thirty dollars a week in support. Dad got the car and unlimited visitation. From then on, we saw Dad when we would run into him at the Club, which my mother now tried to avoid, but because she was alone and without a car and because the club was a walk, but a long one, that allowed her to get away from us, it was her only social activity.

My parents have since gone on to celebrate their golden wedding anniversary and sixty-fifth anniversary as if the divorce had not occurred, and I have never brought it up. Given the short period of time it covered, it was convenient to expunge it from the family record. My brother Dick, who endured that black period along with me, can recall nothing of it. In my life, however, it has its searing place. Incidental as the episode seemed to have been and even though the families did their best to remove all traces of its effect, for me it was a shot in the heart.

Life went on for us. My father moved out, and we remained in the apartment. My mother pined after my father; my father had second thoughts about the breakup. My mother's situation was perilous, more so than she realized. Abandoned, so to speak, in a city, my "handicapped" mother had no marketable skills whatever, owned no car and couldn't drive anyway, and was expected to live on a generous but still meager amount of alimony and child support. It didn't take long for the realities of being alone in the city to make her aware that her only salvation lay in another marriage or in a reconciliation.

For a time, Mom went out with Ralph Lin Weber, a well-to-do courtly bachelor who was hard of hearing and, so, existed in the middle ground between the Deaf and the Hearing communities. For many minor-league baseball aficionados, he is remembered as the preeminent historian of the Toledo Mud Hens and an assiduous collector of baseball memorabilia. I discovered he died only recently, in 1997. Mom would occasionally put the question to us as to whether she should marry Mr. Lin Weber or reconcile with Dad, and of course, we chose our dad—another one of Mom's meaningless questions.

Yet, the genuine affection Mom and Dad felt for each other was never far from the surface, and the divorce was clearly a mistake. From Christmas of 1944 onward, my parents had begun seeing each other again, and the change in their relationship was one that Dick and I greeted ecstatically. As I deduced from official records, apparently sometime in late January or early February of 1945, my mother must have discovered she was pregnant, and remarriage followed within four months of the finalization of the divorce. On March 7, 1945, Richard and Elizabeth Miller remarried, and the remarriage was followed by the arrival on October 18 of my brother Arthur Ray, named after my grandfather Sowers.

A year and three months later came the birth of my youngest brother, John Adam, after a difficult pregnancy and traumatic delivery. My mother has always been extremely sensitive to pain, and she insisted that she be anesthetized as she had been for Art's birth, but apparently, that demand made an already difficult delivery all the more difficult, and John was the victim. He suffered from oxygen deprivation, which left him slightly learning impaired and probably led to the ruptured cranial aneurysm he suffered in 1998 and his death in 2002. In spite of these adversities, he lived a full life, was a Vietnam-era veteran of the Army, married, and worked in the same factory with Dad until 1998 when he became disabled.

The hasty reconciliation suggests a reason for the tension in my parents' marriage. My parents' sexual knowledge was so primitive at the time that problems in the marriage seemed to grow out of my mother's decision, probably fueled by Grandma Sowers, to stop sexual relations after Dick was born, when Mom was 22 and Dad 23. Mom told me recently that, later, after the fourth child John was born, Grandma Sowers gave my dad a stern lecture about bringing on all these pregnancies, which meant by any understanding that Grandma Sowers, like many of her generation, preached old-fashioned abstinence, the nineteenth-century "closing of the bedroom door." She had no sympathy with Margaret Sanger and birth-control advocates. Whatever my parents' problems may have been, I believe this tragedy was initiated by Hearing parents either too ignorant about sex themselves to provide sensible advice or only too happy to bring this dangerous childbearing to an end. That benighted attitude was seconded by an institutional upbringing that had not prepared them in any way for the practical problems of marriage.

But the divorce, which we had chased away into a dark corner of our lives, was only the beginning of a period of unceasing pain that didn't end until 1954 when Mom and Dad were finally able to find steady jobs and begin the steep climb out of poverty. An even darker episode came with the end of the war in 1945. It was the beginning of the most depressing period of my life and the life of the family, and it came as Mom and Dad were putting their lives back together after the divorce. With the decline in demand for war materiel, particularly the Jeep, which was produced in the Toledo plant, and the return of soldiers to reclaim their jobs, Dad was laid off permanently. We were thrown back on the charity of relatives and the meager unemployment compensation available at the time. Mom joined the workforce while Dad stayed home with us four boys and fretted. The country had used the willing labor of Deaf people and then hung them out to dry. I really didn't understand the full meaning of those cataclysmic economic times until I read Robert M. Buchanan's *Illusions of Equality: Deaf Americans in School and Factory 1850–1950*[2] in which he discusses the widespread hardship that beset the Deaf community after the war.

So here were my parents with two young boys and two new babies, a mountain of debt, and no prospects of work. Dad stayed in the apartment and tried to be the dutiful househusband, or he went out looking for work. Mom felt increasingly frustrated as our situation got more and more desperate. Night after night, we all sat around like the Micawbers, hoping that something would turn up.

---

2. Washington, DC: Gallaudet University Press, 1999.

At last, Dad found work. He got hired by the DeVilbiss Company, a manufacturer of paint-spraying equipment, but periodically he was laid off and back on unemployment. As soon as the two little boys were big enough, Mom got a job at the Variety Club Bottling Company and, more often than not, was the breadwinner in the family. Dad became the short-tempered father that I remember only with pain. This change of roles did not sit well at all. Every day, the scene repeated itself: Mom and Dad would bicker over money, then the tears, arguments over bills due, and agonizing sessions in which decisions would have to be made about whom to pay, if anyone. Had it not been for the help of my grandparents Sowers and hundreds of Kraft dinners, we'd never have made it. I haven't touched a Kraft dinner in forty-five years and never ate macaroni and cheese casserole when it was served in the dining hall at college. Nevertheless, in spite of the

Miller family, Toledo, Ohio, 1949. Front: Bob, Art, Dick; rear: Mom, Dad, John.

tensions, the marriage held. For a time, Dad found work in the shoe repair department of a local department store, but it paid poorly, and we were desperate.

Finally, the combination of Dad's not being able to find a decent job, the constant trouble Dick and I got into, and perhaps the stigma of the divorce and remarriage forced a change. Both sets of grandparents were convinced that Dick and I were headed for juvenile delinquency, and perhaps they were right. Dick was constantly getting hit by cars and getting into scrapes. The most serious came when he and a friend were refused free potato chips at the local potato chip factory (I think it was called Siford's). They decided to get even by setting fire to the roof of the factory and did it—and also got caught.

Mom and Dad were beside themselves. Something had to be done, and soon. The combination of the job market and the increasing difficulty of bringing up four boys in the city pushed them closer to a fateful decision—to move back to the farm. Their parents couldn't understand the poignancy of that decision because they saw the city as the root of all our problems when, in fact, the city with its large Deaf population was the nurturing environment on which my parents depended.

One night when my parents are entertaining friends, I am running a high fever and am put to bed in their room to be isolated from my brothers. As I lie there in the dark, I reach up above my head and discover I can just manage to twirl the dial of the safe. The wall safe in my parents' bedroom attracts no end of interest from all of us, Mom and Dad included. We are always fiddling with the dial to see whether we can open it. It has become the altar upon which we place our hopes and dreams. We are convinced that it holds some great treasure and that opening it will be like winning the lottery, the answer to all our troubles.

After a couple of hours of spinning and turning, I hear a click, and then the dial locks in place. My heart races, I get out of bed and call my parents, and they in turn hustle their friends into the bedroom to open the safe. Dad is given the honors and carefully draws the door open to reveal—nothing. It is empty. I have destroyed our future.

In the end, my clever dad dopes out the mechanism of the safe, resets the combination, and we use it to store personal papers until we move away and lock it up to be a puzzle and a symbol of hope for the next tenant. As Dad closes it for the last time, out of some perverse sense of outrage, I manage to sneak a piece of tablet paper into it with the message, "SURPRISE!!!"

Over time, the neighborhood becomes part of a spreading Black ghetto, and then finally, all the apartment buildings are razed as part of the urban renewal efforts of the 1960s. I wonder what happened to that safe, I wonder whether anyone got the message?

In the fall of 1949, Mom and Dad settled on a plan to move us all back to Defiance to the farm—for Mom and Dad to move back into their old half of the farmhouse and for Dad to take up once again his place as a share partner with his stepfather, my Grandpa Lloyd Newton, in the dairy farming business. Mom, who hated the farm with a passion, considered the plan a bitter defeat because she thrived on city life, on the shops, the movie theaters, the Deaf community, her Silent Club. I was excited about moving back to the farm—to live next door to my favorite grandparents, to resurrect the country life and all those wonderful memories I had of it. Little did I know then that for me, too, things were not about to get better, but much worse.

5 Back on the Farm (1950–1953)

CHRISTMAS 1949 was the worst—the bleakest Christmas of my life. Dick and I had grown used to big Christmases while Dad was bringing home a good paycheck. During the fat years, my parents, indulging their childlike infatuation with all the goodies that Christmas brings, gladly went into hock to shower presents on their two little boys, on relatives and friends, and on themselves. Now, with Dad out of work and two more boys in the family, Christmases had gotten leaner and leaner. By this Christmas, we were down to gifts of blue jeans and socks as well as other items that we could use in our move to the farm. Dad still had his fabulous tree, which he turned into a work of art as usual, and as usual, we were not allowed to put even one decoration on it. A couple of years earlier, after Dad had spent hours creating his masterpiece, Dick and I brought it crashing down when we were horsing around, diving off the couch into cushions. A memorable Christmas that one was indeed.

We spent our meager holiday in Toledo and then packed for the move to Defiance so we could change schools at midyear. For some weeks, my parents had been making the sixty-mile trip to the farm to get our new digs ready. They tried to make the musty rooms in the farmhouse take on some decent resemblance to the airy apartment Mom had grown fond of in Toledo, but no amount of wallpaper or paint could change them.

On that cold winter day, we climbed out of the car and entered our side of the house. The rooms were freezing and bare, and even though the oil stove had been turned on, it couldn't seem to dispel the feeling of alienation I sensed in that house. Somehow, I realized on the spot that this country life was not going to reprise the idyllic holiday weekends and summers I used to spend at my grandparents' place.

From the comfort of our modest city apartment, we moved to the spare facilities of a house built in the late nineteenth century, split into two living spaces with no central heat and no indoor toilet. Each side of the house mirrored the other somewhat. On our side, on the ground floor was a kitchen, pantry, spare room, and living room, with a hallway and stairs leading to the second floor. Upstairs were two bedrooms and closets, the smaller for my parents and the larger holding two double beds in which we four boys slept, I with my brother Art and Dick with John. The arrangement was settled on because Dick and I fought constantly.

Our side of the house was heated by a fuel oil stove, which sat in the living room and usually ran on the highest setting because Mom was always cold. Heat for the upstairs wafted through the stairwell or through a small floor vent in our bedroom. At night, when my parents had company and we would be sent to bed, we would all hover over the floor vent and peer down into the kitchen and try to make out what was going on. But it was fruitless; there was nothing to hear, and we couldn't see their hands well enough to eavesdrop.

Toilet facilities were "out back" in a shed just behind the house, where coal for Grandma's kitchen stove as well as rakes, hoes, scythes, and the like were stored and where a partition with a door gave privacy to a one-hole privy. We took our baths once a week in the kitchen in a laundry tub. My grandparents had indoor plumbing on their side of the house, so if I needed a good bath for a special occasion, Grandma would let me use their bathroom. Several years later, when I was in college, my parents put in a bathroom, and then only because Mom's parents generously gave them the money to pay for it. Of course, to cut expenses, Dad did all the work himself.

I was eleven at the time of our move from Toledo, still too young to take on a lot of work responsibility, but my parents and grandparents made it very clear to me that I was expected to pull my weight, which began with light chores.

Grandma Amy and Grandpa Lloyd, c. 1954.

Within a few days, after we've settled in, Grandma takes me aside and tells me, "Bobby, you're big enough now to help out around here. Dad and Grandpa have some chores you need to do. Now I want you to keep the waterers filled in the chicken coop every morning and evening, and in the afternoon when you're not in school, you can gather the eggs. Later, when you get the hang of that, your dad will show you how to slop the hogs." Our egg production is headed not for the groceries but the chick hatchery, and so our flock is made up of roosters and hens, Barred Plymouth Rock roosters and Rhode Island Red hens, to produce a hybrid bird for the meat market.

I slink off to my chores shorn of my illusions about farm life.

As I cross the chicken yard, I feel a huge WHAP and a sharp stab in the calf of my leg. I turn around and see a large, very irate rooster about to give me a second flopping. Off for the house I tear with the rooster not far behind me. I jam the gate shut and look up to see Grandma smiling in the kitchen window. She comes out the back door and scolds me, "Come on, Bobby, you're a farm boy now. Don't let that old rooster get the best of you."

I cry, "But Grandma, I'm scared of him. I can't go out there."

She scoffs, "Well, go out there you will because that's what you got to do. So you might as well get used to it."

She returns to her kitchen. I look around and find a short piece of 2x4 that will make a nice club and prepare myself for the fight. I creep into the yard, but the rooster spots me right away, and begins that comical dance with which I am to become all too familiar.

But I'm ready for him. As he races to the attack, I swing the 2x4 and, as they say, "cold-cock" him. He does a small circle dance and falls over dead.

Grandma comes running out of the kitchen, shouting, "Bobby, what in the Lord's name have you done to that chicken! That was one of my prize roosters! Well, you can just learn to clean chickens now."

So it was that I learned to clean chickens, and water chickens, and gather eggs. But whenever I went into the chicken yard I always went armed, although not with so menacing a weapon.

Gathering eggs I hated, because I wound up with peck marks all over the backs of my hands. Besides, egg gathering was considered "woman's work." Eventually, like all my friends, I rose early, did chores, ate breakfast, and then got on the school bus for the hour-plus ride to school. When I got older, I was expected to help with the morning milking, but it was such a hassle for Dad to get me out of bed that he finally gave up the effort and let me have that extra two hours' sleep.

As I had done during my summer visits to the Other Place, I also continued to raise broilers on the side and managed to accumulate a little savings that way. This skill not only made me something of an entrepreneur but also got me appointed the official chicken killer and dresser, a job I would have preferred to forgo. Chickens were dispatched with a cleaver on an upended log. The usual practice was to lop off the head and give the chicken a toss at which point it would flop grotesquely around the yard, spraying blood everywhere. But I devised a technique in which I held onto the ends of the wings and legs and let the blood drain out while I kept the chicken in an iron grip. Everyone on the farm thought the technique very clever, and I got a reputation as something of a humanitarian for my pains.

For me, the move to the farmhouse brought cataclysmic changes. In Toledo, I had had some responsibilities in helping my parents out, but here, I was about to be the prize in a tug-of-war that was to last until I was far along into high school, and I did not handle it well at all. I was to become the go-between for my parents and grand-parents, between two worlds that could barely communicate with each other, whose values were diametrically opposed to each other and could never be reconciled. My baptism into this onerous chore occurred right off the bat.

As usual, I happen to be moping around in the barn, when I notice Dad and Grandpa locked in a furious writing contest as each takes the pad, writes some remark, passes it to the other, and then the same process is repeated. Finally, Grandpa calls to me, "Bob, come on over here and help me explain this to your dad."

Like a dog knowing he's about to get a whipping, I slowly slink over. Grandpa explains what he wants to me. I turn to Dad, and in about five seconds of signing, I pass on the instructions to him. He understands immediately, but I see the resentment and humiliation well up in his eyes. And when I turn to Grandpa, I see a look of relief, as if he's had his prayers answered. I know the die has been cast. I know what my main "job" on the farm will be.

Even at that age, I quickly realized that I had been conned into believing in one of the oldest American myths—that rural is better than urban, the country better than the city—when in reality, the country had turned out to be more callous and cruel than the city. My role model for survival was my parents, living out in the middle of nowhere with the nearest Deaf family more than twenty miles away—and coping. I could see that we had made a terrible mistake, that somehow we should have slugged it out in Toledo, but they had done it, on the advice of their parents, for the family, for their kids, for a better life.

*This evening, after the milking is done and supper over, Mom turns
to Dick and me and says, "Dad got a callback to his job at DeVilbiss and
we're thinking we should go back to Toledo. Would you boys like that?"*

Dad watches us intently.

*I am torn apart. I want to go back, but I don't want to face all the
arguing, the going without, the fighting over bills, the whole insecure
existence I was glad to escape. I say, "Would Dad get laid off again?"*

Dad replies candidly, "I don't know."

*That tears it for me. In the face of two bad choices, Dick and I opt
for the one that seems to promise the more stable life for us.*

Many years later, Mom would tell this story somewhat ruefully
and try to find a way to place the responsibility for that decision on
Dick and me. It was consistent with Mom's habit of putting the blame
on others for bad choices she and Dad had made. Maybe it was unfair.
Given our ages and the choices we had, who would have chosen differently? All I could think was that, bad as life on the farm was, I
wasn't sure I wanted to return to the uncertainties, the poverty, and
domestic wars of Toledo. Our lives had been set on a certain course,
and now we had to make it work. After all my parents had been able
to endure, I thought, how could they not expect their sons to learn
to survive? I had no choice but to suffer on, through many nights of
silent tears. During the day, when I couldn't stand the pressure any
longer, I would steal away to the horse barn, a large building farthest
from the house that was somewhat secluded from the others, and
hide in a "fort" I had made from hay bales up in the haymow. There
I would sit with my legs crossed and follow a kind of meditation
that I fell into naturally. If I looked intensely through a crack in the

barn siding I could see Five Mile Creek, which ran through our pasture, so still and so silent and seemingly so far away and peaceful.

With my grandparents now just a few steps from us on the other side of the wall, so to speak, I knew that, whenever I got into a confrontation with Mom and Dad, I had a refuge, and I was quick to take advantage of it. For a time, I continued to be a fishing companion to Grandpa Lloyd, as I had been during those summers I spent with them when we lived in Toledo. And being a kind of dreamy, cerebral boy, I also liked to sit in Grandma's kitchen and while away the hours in random conversation as she labored to make her preserves, pies, bread, and noodles. My grandparents were indulgent but also discreet, yet inevitably, I picked up on the deep divide that separated them from my parents and their way of life.

Mom and I are having a brutal set-to about whether I will go with them for the day on a visit to some of their Deaf friends who live about twenty-five miles away. Even though Mom can't hear me, I am screaming and repeatedly signing NO! to her insistence that I go, and she is shrieking and signing back at me just as forcefully. I don't want to go because no kids my age are there to play with, and I know that all I'll be able to do is sit on the couch and watch as my parents and their friends enjoy their drawn-out, animated conversations, which will last well into the night.

Finally, I scream at her and sign as forcefully as I can, "You can't make me go, YOU CAN'T!" Mom dives for me but I am quickly out the back door and around the corner and into Grandma's kitchen. Mom doesn't pursue because she doesn't want to make a scene in front of Grandma, and I know it.

Grandma asks, "What on earth is going on, Bobby?"

I answer, "Oh, Mom wants me to go to their dumb ol' friends' house and I don't want to go there and stand around and watch them talk. Half of what they say I can't understand and the rest I'm not interested in. It's so boring!"

Quickly she admonishes me, "Now, you know it's not nice to talk about folks like that!"

"Well, I don't care. I just don't want to go!"

She hesitates, then slowly frames a careful reply, "I have to say, sometimes I wish your folks wouldn't be on the go so much, what with all the expense and such. I wish they'd just stay around here more. All that gas money. It's a shame to see it all go down the drain."

Deep within me, a feeling of resentment wells up at her criticism of Mom and Dad. Somehow, I sense that it's all wrong, what I've done, that I've crossed a line and I need to get back.

As Grandma is busy putting a pie in the oven I sneak out the door and go back to face Mom and tell her I'll go.

And so the war went on. Mom and Dad would go to almost any lengths to keep up the bond between themselves and their Deaf circle or, rather, Mom would, and Dad would often follow just to keep the peace. I would complain, quarrel with them, "Why are we spending all this money on gas, on the car, when we need to pay bills?" I was completely out of line, and my parents were enraged at what they took to be smart-aleck behavior from their disrespectful son. My mother would be in my face with her two-sign retort, "Think smart!" ("You think you're so smart!"), and I'd back off. I hadn't a clue to what it all meant to them. They were Deaf, I was

Hearing, and I expected them to give up their needs, just like that. It was a vain expectation, and I had no right to insist on it.

At home, I was entering my teen years in an environment where I was torn between my love for my parents as well as my desire to respect them and a Hearing world that viewed them altogether differently and that demanded allegiance from me. As I grew up, I became more and more alienated from my parents, which is natural as we assert our independence, but I also was growing less and less comfortable with my parents and their Deaf world, which daily became less my world as I began to recognize that my life lay in the land of the Hearing. The experience is one common to all CODAs, who, if they deny it, are denying the very conflict that defines them. The CODAs of my generation were born into a Hearing world that drew us increasingly away from our Deaf parents, that instilled in us a revulsion to their speech and to their folkways, which were the result of deprived childhoods and inadequate education that manifested in their own parenting. What makes my experience of this alienation all the more poignant is that I felt it almost daily in the close quarters of Deaf and Hearing family association.

Mom had always hated the farming life, but she did her best to cope, and Dad put all his effort into once more attending to the back-breaking chores of a dairy farm—milking twice a day, looking after the stock, washing up after the milking— and in the summer, the haymaking, the field work, and in the fall, the harvesting. Most onerous to him was having to deal with his stepfather (referred to in sign language as "Father Third," meaning third after his father Miller and his stepfather Shank), who communicated with him either by shouting in a futile attempt to make him hear (no point trying to explain to Grandpa that shouting was futile) or through painstaking, semiliterate, often confusing written instructions Grandpa prepared every morning after the milking. My first task was to try to figure out what it was Grandpa had written in his instructions. Then, as always, my task was to serve as interpreter and, too often, as mediator between the two of them. Neither Grandpa Lloyd nor Grandma Amy had command of a single sign and had no desire to try to learn any of them. It was almost as if they were afraid of actually being able to talk to Mom and Dad.

Usually, communication took place at a kind of council of war in the milk house, where the parts of the milking machine, buckets, and strainers were washed and placed on racks and where the ten-gallon cans of milk were stored in a cooler waiting to be picked up twice a week by the milk truck. The milk house was a kind of social center of the working part of the farm because it had a coal stove to which in wintertime, especially in those sub-zero northern Ohio winters, we all retreated. It was a place where you could smoke; smoking was not allowed in the barns, and Dad was a smoker then. Grandpa could take time for a chew from a pouch of his favorite stuff, Bagpipe chewing tobacco, which I would occasionally sneak a wad of and just as regularly get sick to my stomach from.

My chore every morning was to fire up the stove to heat the water for washing the milkers. On one occasion, I almost burned down the building when I was soldering a bucket and laid the iron on the ledge of a wall that was covered on the inside with tarpaper. Flames leapt up the wall, but I quickly doused them with water from the pump in the washroom and then tacked up some fresh tarpaper, and no one ever noticed. Fire was the one thing all farmers feared, especially dairy farmers, with those old barns of well-seasoned wood full of dried hay. Once a barn caught fire, it would be reduced to a pile of ashes within minutes, as I had occasion to witness twice at other farms.

Grandpa, Dad, and I gather in the milk house to map out the day's work. The weather is brutally cold, the little coal stove throws its heat across the room, but it dissipates before it reaches the icy walls. I stare at the thin red crescents of fire I can see around the two cast iron lids on its surface.

Grandpa has written out instructions to Dad to take some fencing over to the "krik" and the word looks to Dad like "krib," meaning to him the corncrib out beyond the horse barn. We spend the better part of the morning loading fencing supplies and then unloading them near the crib.

The next morning, Grandpa is furious with Dad, and then asks me why we didn't take the fence posts over to the "crick" (that is, "creek").

Dad hurls the pad across the room in disgust, and stalks off to begin the work of the day.

Grandpa makes some slur about Dad being dumb, which is always an incendiary word with me because of the old "deaf-and-dumb" phrase that is always on the tip of everyone's tongue.

I scream at him, "God damn it, you can't say that! You can't say that! He's my DAD!" We are both shocked, and I run out of the milk house in tears. Nothing is ever said about it, and it never happens again.

This unholy trio of Dad, Grandpa Lloyd, and me had certain dynamics built into it that compromised deeply my relationship with my father. In my role as interpreter, I was "management" because my task was to deliver "orders" and to convey criticisms and general bitches, which were frequent. My father was placed in the position of being humiliated by proxy by his own son. It was a horrible position for me to be in and was made worse by Grandpa Lloyd's desperate need to have a son, a boy that had been denied to him.

When we mow the hay into the barn, we use grappling forks to grasp the small round bales that are the precursors of the large bales that are to become popular in future years. The forks clutch the bales; the tractor pulls the rope that, through a series of pulleys, draws the forks up and into the upper part of the barn in the haymow, where a man calls out a signal. The tractor stops, the forks are tripped, and the bales drop to the floor. Then customarily, the forks are pulled by hand back out of the barn, they trip and drop onto the hay wagon to be placed around another load of bales.

Grandpa Lloyd wants to be a part of the haymaking, yet he cannot possibly draw the forks out by hand, so he ties the pulling rope to the bumper of his old Plymouth, backs it up and pulls the forks out that way. The problem is, he is hard of hearing, has a slippery clutch foot, and has a heavy accelerator foot, a bad combination.

I drive the tractor and pull up a load of bales. The man in the mow calls out the signal, I stop, Dad trips the forks, and the bales drop to the floor of the mow as slick as you could wish.

Then comes the hard part. Grandpa revs up the Plymouth, his foot slips off the clutch, the car lurches backward at a wicked speed, the forks come flying out of the barn and sail through the air over the wagon and onto the ground about two feet from one of the workers. Grandpa gets out of the car and yells, "Goddammit, that kid (meaning me) was supposed to let me know when the forks was coming out! Bob, why don't you watch your business?"

I don't say anything, but Dad asks me what Grandpa said, and I explain. Dad smiles, and signs to me, "I guess he must be deaf—and dumb!"

As the battle lines got drawn I became more and more Dad's advocate, and I used my position to defend him, to pose arguments and explanations that he often was not aware of. Over time, Grandpa

Lloyd, who was no slouch when it came to clever dealing, began to tumble to my game and sensed a conspiracy in the making. What saved this situation from exploding into a major crisis was, first, Dad's stoical bearing, patience, and sound judgment. The second element was the growing pressure of economic realities that would finally force this so-called partnership to end.

Grandma communicated by way of speechreading, which Dad was quite good at. She would mouth her words to him, or if she had something particularly complicated to tell either Mom or Dad, she might fall back on pad and pencil. But usually, I would be called in to explain. She was much the gentler one, a woman of great tact and goodness, known throughout the farming community for her kindliness, but still, her disapproval was often a palpable thing. Needless to say, any misunderstandings that might occur were blamed on Bobby, by both parties.

During these years, Dad and I got along well and a camaraderie grew between us. Being a farm kid, I was always out there with him, helping in the field and helping in the barns. Dad was the understanding boss who knew what it was to have to slave under a master, so he always treated me well, in fact, better than I deserved. If I got rebellious, he most likely would fall into his usual passive-aggressive mode and say, "Okay, I'll do it myself," and I would be shamed into doing my work. I tried this technique on my own teenagers for a time, but they soon called my bluff, and I caved.

It is late May. In preparation for storing hay, Dad climbs up into the highest peak of what we call the horse barn, a remnant of the Newton horse-breeding days, and changes the rope pulleys and the "car" through which the ropes pass, all of which controls the travel of the hayforks.

First, the two of us climb up the ladder into the hay mow, and then Dad continues on up a ladder attached to the end wall, which leads to a kind of crow's nest fashioned of 2x4s that surround the window in the peak of the gable of the barn roof where the pulley is anchored by a chain attached to a beam in the peak. To reach the pulley wheel and remove it so it can be moved to the opposite gable of the barn, Dad wraps his legs around a 2x4, hangs onto a rope with one hand, and leans out in space. Then with the other hand, he catches tools and parts that I toss up in the air to him.

Down below me, on the ground floor in the center of the barn, I see Grandpa watching, enthralled.

No matter how often Dad "surprised" Grandpa with his intelligence or his extraordinary skills, Grandpa never seemed to be able to grasp the truth that Deaf people were simply Hearing people who could not hear, whose intellectual development was hindered by the privations brought on by delayed and limited language development and by poor schooling. In terms of intelligence, Dad was clearly ten miles down the road ahead of Grandpa, whose own schooling was limited, whose language skills were extremely poor, and whose math skills were just as bad.

While my feelings for and connection with Dad grew stronger by the day, my relations with Mom were awful, and they got even worse. Unlike Dad, she had a violent temper and a short fuse that led to it. She also suffered from a deep-seated sense of inferiority because she couldn't measure up as the model farm wife and from her seeming lack of intelligence, which, in all honesty, Dad was sometimes quick to reinforce. Both of us still have a habit of being impatient and patronizing with anyone who doesn't "get it" right away, as my wife and kids have pointed out to me many times. Her unhappiness with the farm life, her loneliness, her sometimes appalling lack of good judgment, and her rages all fed my natural desire to rebel, so as I entered my teen years, I found myself almost constantly at odds with Mom.

Call it midlife crisis or what you will, Mom had entered what I now jokingly refer to as her Bottle Blonde phase. She began bleaching her hair in a fashion that had been made popular by Marilyn Monroe and other stars of the '50s and '60s. (After 1953, when both Mom and Dad were fully employed and the money was coming in, she tore loose on a clothes-buying spree that has only slowed in recent years.) I still have an image of her with her hair down, naked from the waist up except for her bra, bent over the kitchen sink (no bathroom yet), dipping and dabbing from the peroxide bottle. Somehow, the little girl within, deprived of hearing, deprived of home and parents for much of her youth, was still screaming for attention.

Initially, my parents had to time all their trips, including drives to Mom's family in Fostoria, between the morning and evening milking, and my parents never took a vacation during the years the farm was active. In all the years I knew my grandparents, they took only two vacations, once to visit a cousin in North Carolina and once to take a trip with Uncle Lester and his family. For us, big trips meant the Toledo Zoo, Geauga Lake, Indian Lake, or, if we really got lucky, Cedar Point, mecca of all northern Ohio kids. I once remarked to my kids that I had never been out of the state of Ohio until I was seventeen, and it is true. They were stunned. For an outing to, say, Cedar Point, which was about a two-hour-plus drive, we would get out extra early, do all the chores, pile into the car, get there and frantically ride all the rides and swim in Lake Erie, then ride back exhausted to face the evening milking and chores and work late into the night. And my grandparents watched all this gallivanting with deep disapproval because they knew my parents would come back out of cash and have to struggle through the weeks to come.

As I grew older and more expert at handling the cows, I was finally allowed to do the milking on my own, which gave my parents a little freedom. Cedar Point I hated to miss, but trips to Fostoria I would gladly pass up. My first experience at doing the milking by myself happened when Mom and Dad and my three brothers took the day trip to Fostoria while I stayed behind because, as I said, I found visits to my Fostoria grandparents terminally boring. That morning, Dad took me through all the steps of the procedure.

In the evening, I go out to start the milking. I herd the cows up from the pasture, with the help of our dog Sugar, and shut them in the barnyard. I open the barn to let the cows in to their assigned stanchions, which they know how to pick out routinely. The cows walk in, but they won't enter their stanchions, and I have fifteen crazed cows milling about in the milking area. I run them back out into the barnyard and puzzle and puzzle. I have to do something quick. I've got all these cows to milk, and it's getting late, and if I don't get on with it, some of them might come down with mastitis. Then, Eureka, it comes to me. I forgot to put feed in the trough that runs in front of the stanchions. Quickly, I put the feed out and run the cows in to the milking area. They each go to their stanchions slick as goose grease, as we'd say on the farm. I am saved. My parents come home late that night, and Dad marvels at what a good job I've done on my own.

After the move from Toledo, it took some time for Dick and me to put down roots and link up with kids our age. Fortunately, we had a large family next to us on the Schatz farm, and Marv Schatz, who was a year younger than I, became my best friend throughout all those years, which, at times, must have been very trying given that I was a pariah during the early days at Sherry School and then Defiance Township School. The Ed Schatz family was an extended family like ours, with Ed, his wife Mildred, and kids living in the larger part of the house and Ed's mother and his maiden sister Helen living in the smaller part of it. Their family was soon to be reduced by one with the death of sister Dorothy, at age three, from rheumatic fever.

Marv buddied around with me, and his brother John, with my brother Dick, until John came down with a severe case of polio during the epidemic and was moved for treatment to Toledo where he remained for more than a year. The disease rendered him a paraplegic, but he went on to become a high school teacher and is now retired and living in Defiance. When we weren't all playing baseball until absolute pitch dark, we were busy figuring out some kind of devilment to practice on Aunt Helen.

In addition to Marv and me, the third member of our unholy trio was Louie Peiffer, the youngest in a family of four who was actually an only child because his two sisters and brother had already reached adulthood and gone on their own. Louie and his parents occupied a small house on the Hammersmith Road, not too far from us. Marv had shown real gifts and had been moved up a grade, and Louie, too, was a very bright kid. In adulthood, true to our early potential, we all left the farm and ended up in professions.

What made these two guys, and their families as well, so precious to me was that they totally accepted my parents' Deafness and felt completely at home in our family, which was a great relief after so many times when I would bring friends home, introduce them to my parents, and then see them put off by what they considered to be weird people. Children can be the cruelest when they display their reactions openly, and whenever I would bring a friend over, I would have to go through a routine explaining to them about my Deaf parents. I had a speech all worked out: "I gotta tell you, before we go in, my parents are Deaf, you know? That means they can't hear, so when they talk, they talk kinda funny, but it's OK, you'll like them." Sometimes they did, sometimes they didn't, and sometimes they did until they went home and told their parents about the Miller kid's Deaf folks, and then they didn't. It was doubly painful for me because Mom and Dad were open, happy, welcoming, and giving people who were eager for us to be accepted.

6   Sherry School (1950)

Sometime in January 1950, several weeks after we have moved from Toledo to the farm, I am headed to the schoolyard at Sherry School. As I move to get off the bus, I feel a hard shove and grab the side rails along the steps to keep from rolling out the bus door and into the slush and mud of the drive. No one looks at me, no one shows any signs of guilt.

The school looms gray and forbidding in the early dawn, like Lowood School in Jane Eyre, *its belfry prominent against the treeless horizon. I go in, hang up my coat, put my lunchbox on the shelf, and go to my seat. I see one of the Nelson kids bent over another desk close by. Mrs. Custer, our teacher, is busy outside, herding kids in for the opening of the day. The Nelson kid turns to me, puts his mouth next to my right ear, and says, "Hey, Miller, CAN YOU HEAR ME? HAHAHAHA!" I come up from my seat swinging and graze his chin. He hits me with a powerful blow to my right ear, the ear that always has infections, and the tears well up in*

*my eyes. But I manage to hold them back. I can feel the ache begin deep
inside my head, and I know it will develop into a full-blown earache.*

Mrs. Custer comes in and says, "What's going on in here?"

No one says a word, especially not me.

When we moved back to the farm, I had no idea what kind of
school I would be attending. I had been coddled by an urban education that included field trips to museums, concerts, firehouses, and
police stations and that also included structured playtime, educational
assemblies, and one of the best physical facilities in the city. What a
surprise was in store for me when I stepped off the bus to see Sherry
School, a one-room, dilapidated, clapboard building with a belfry but
no bell and, out back, two rickety, unpainted outhouses, one for each
sex. The schoolhouse was heated by a coal stove cased in a metal
jacket, which was fired up each morning by Bud Rohlf, an eighth-
grader who lived close by. The four older grades were taught at Sherry,
and the four younger ones at Kiser School. Because I was in the sixth
grade, I attended Sherry while Dick, in the fourth grade, went to Kiser.

Today, Sherry School has been restored and is now on display at the
Auglaize Village Museum, off U.S. 24 west of Defiance, on Krouse
Road. I happened to spot it one day in the 1970s when I was driving around the countryside with my wife and children. We stopped
and went inside it, and I showed them where I had sat in sixth
grade. I have to confess, they were mightily underwhelmed.

*One afternoon at recess, as I am walking past some seventh graders,
I catch a little bit of their conversation, which goes something like this*

Sherry school (restored), Auglaize Village, Defiance, Ohio, c. 1975.

(in low tones): "There's that Miller kid, he's got them deef-and-dumb folks, you know, they can't hear."

Another kid: "Yeah, more dumb than deef I hear. Ha, ha, get it? 'I hear'?" At that point, I jump the garbage-mouth and promptly get the shit kicked out of me.

After a while, once the kids got the message that, even if I got knocked around, I wasn't going to take the insults, they stopped. If I hadn't stood my ground, their tortures would have gotten worse. True to my nature, which I shared with my dad, I was not a fighter, but I learned soon enough that, if you were going to survive or at least have a tolerable life at that school, you had to be willing to fight, even if you lost every fight you got into, and I lost quite a few.

On that first school day in January, Dick and I were put on the bus in the dark. We rode together for more than an hour, objects of curiosity, until I was let off at Sherry and Dick was taken on to Kiser. Mom had cleaned us up, put nice city clothes on us, and generally dandified us for this first appearance, and the result was a disaster. All the other kids showed up in tattered jeans, denim jackets, cotton gloves, and farm shoes, or clodhoppers (from which comes the slang term for farmers)—kind of a grunge style before grunge had become fashionable. The kids set on me immediately and never let up. To make things worse, I was blocked from using the toilet by some of the older kids, and before the end of the day, I had peed in my pants, but I managed to hide the fact from everyone, including Mrs. Custer, our teacher. I got home undetected, took off my pants and shorts in the pump house, rinsed them out in the cattle tank (this in January!) and made up some phony story to tell my parents about falling in a snow bank. I was not looking forward to the next day. And there were lots of "next days" before things changed.

Sherry School was primitive in many ways. Its bow to technology was a blackboard, a few old maps, and portraits of Washington and Lincoln. This center of culture, which is really all we had by way of culture, was a long way away from the school, art museum, and public library I had been able to escape to in Toledo. All four grades were in the one room, with about five to six students in each grade. We sat at wooden double desks with inkwells that were not used now that ballpoint pens had been invented. We carried our lunches in metal lunch boxes that held thermoses of milk in their deep lids and kept them on shelves at the back of the schoolroom. We hung our coats on pegs also at the back of the room, and during snowy winter days, we laid our cheap, cotton work gloves to dry over the edge of the metal jacket that surrounded the coal stove. One of the popular pranks was to flip the gloves over the edge and onto the stove where they would smolder for a time and, then, usually in the middle of the school period, smoke violently, and then Mrs. Custer would have to evacuate the school and have one of the eighth-grade boys (they always got to do all the neat stuff) retrieve the offending glove, and then, the building would have to be aired out and heated up again. School was never dismissed early because we had no way to get home until the two buses showed up.

School began at 7:45 and proceeded through lessons, a morning recess, a lunch period, an afternoon recess, and more lessons before it closed at 3:45. During spring planting and fall harvest, kids were allowed to be absent so they could help out on the farm, but my parents would never permit it. School always came first. In a nod to progressive education, students who were advancing rapidly were allowed to "move up" for certain subjects, so I was eventually allowed to do arithmetic and English with the students in the next grade up. My buddy Marv Schatz had been put up a whole grade at some point.

One of our cultural activities (there were two) consisted of coloring "hectographed" pictures, reproduced by a primitive pre-mimeograph process; then a contest would be held and Mrs. Custer would pick a winner, always a girl. "Guys" did not win coloring contests, a rule Mrs. Custer understood. The second was the read-aloud period, which came at the end of the day. Every kid looked forward to this time when Mrs. Custer would read to us for about twenty minutes, usually from an adventure novel. Our favorites were the books about the Walton boys. (Anyone remember *The Walton Boys and Rapids Ahead?*) This period was the highlight of the day, and as Mrs. Custer read to us (she was an excellent reader), every child in that room would listen intently to every word, every nuance in her voice. Then the buses would drive up, Mrs. Custer would close her book, and the spell would be broken.

In the spring during recesses, we played ball, which I was never much good at because of my blind eye. One day as I was walking out to shag flies, someone yelled at me, and I turned around and got whacked in my good eye by a line drive that caught up with me as I was crossing the pitcher's mound. My eye swelled shut, but I had to be kept at school and get my eye bathed with cold water because there was no phone or any means of transportation to take me home or to the hospital. At the end of the day, completely blinded by this time because my eye had swelled shut, I was led to the bus, and I rode home. When I arrived, my parents were in shock. They rushed me to town for emergency care. Fortunately, my sight was not affected. In fact, had I not turned around I might have been killed. The experience gave me a taste of what to expect if something were to happen to my good eye. But everyone took the mishap in stride and returned to playing ball the next day—all but me. Within a week, though, I was back at the game because I loved it in spite of my ineptitude and because I knew that, to survive in that school, I had to play the game.

Two groups of us have been hurling ice balls at one another through two open windows in the belfry. When recess ends, Mrs. Custer, in keeping with her normal practice, goes to one of these windows, sticks her head out, and yells, "School time!" as a signal for us all go in to our desks. To our horror, she manages only the first word before WHAP, she gets nailed directly on the forehead by an ice ball and drops like a stone. What is to be done? Fortunately, almost all of us farm kids know how to drive a car, even at the age of eleven or twelve, so Floyd Ankney, the biggest kid in the school (who is almost sixteen and still in the eighth grade), gets the privilege, and he is joined by an honor guard of ragtag kids as they set off for Defiance Hospital with our comatose teacher propped up in the back seat. The rest of us do our homework until the buses come to pick us up, and we ride to our homes as if it were the close of another school day.

The next morning, Mrs. Custer is back at her desk with a handsome shiner but full of high spirits and ready for another day with her impish charges.

At the outset, my grades, especially in arithmetic, were disastrous. What was being covered in the sixth grade here was comparable to the seventh grade in Toledo. Even though these kids were rough, they were very smart and competitive, and schoolwork was taken very seriously. Gone were the nourishing techniques of Warren School. In their place were spelling bees and cipher-downs.

Mrs. Custer explained to Mom and Dad that my schooling in Toledo was a grade behind, and I would have to do some catching up or be put back a grade—so much for the family's little genius. Gradually, though, I adjusted, and gradually, I got caught up until I was no longer the joke of the class but back in front. As I look back, it must have been a major feat to make up the work. I owe my success in no small part to the best teacher I ever had, Lucille Custer, who kept order among those rough farm kids without ever touching one hair of their heads. She was very gifted, she knew what made kids tick, and she loved to have eager students in her classes. Now that I am a teacher myself, I can only say that, as an educator, she was a magician. Quickly, she saw that I had ability, and she fed it. By the close of the school year, I was back in Mom's good graces and, as far as I could be considering that I was a city kid, I was one of the boys. But I had paid a price.

In that school we honored an oath of omerta (silence) more sacred than that of any criminal society: You just never told anyone, particularly a grownup, anything. Consequently, I hid everything and revealed nothing to either my teacher or my parents. If Mom or

Lucille Custer, on the Sherry School grounds, c. 1949. Photo by Louis Custer.

Dad asked how school was going, I said, "Fine," but the truth was that I was the most miserable kid alive, or at least, I thought so. Suicide would have been a welcome choice if I had had any idea of how to go about it. I had no friends, I was doing poorly in school, and I was trying to adapt to a new life with tremendous responsibilities, at least for an eleven-year-old. And as soon as the word got around about my parents, I was to become the target of every kind of insult that could degrade them. In fairness, I have to say that almost all my schoolmates were very welcoming to my parents, but it took only a few tough kids and the acquiescence of others to turn every school day into a living hell.

At the close of the first six weeks of my schooling at Sherry, Mrs. Custer passes out our grade cards and then gives us a stern lecture on showing

the cards to our parents, getting their signatures, and then returning the cards. Some kids snicker. I brace for the bad news, and it is truly bad. In Toledo, I never received traditional grades, only S, U, and O (Satisfactory, Unsatisfactory, and Outstanding) and mostly Os. As she passes the card to me, she gives me a very sad look, and I know the worst is about to happen. I open the card briefly and through blurred, teary eyes I see the rows of Ds and Fs.

What am I going to do? I think of "losing" the card, mislaying it, or any number of lame excuses for not having it. It doesn't occur to me to forge their signatures, which the small cadre of weak students do all the time. But in the end, I decide to face Mom.

At home, I hand the card over to her. She opens it and screams in her shrieking voice, "WHAT? WHAT? WHAT YOU DO IN SCHOOL, YOU ARE A LAZY BOY, SHAME ON YOU, YOU DO SUCH POOR WORK IN YOUR SCHOOL!"

I cower, fully expecting to be hit, but instead, she shakes me and threatens me with the loss of all kinds of privileges I never had anyway. I hold back tears.

Dad stands looking at me and says nothing. Then he takes the card and signs it and gives it back to me.

Even today, I continue to have ambivalent feelings about my mother's incessant drive to push me to succeed. On the one hand, it brings on some exceedingly painful feelings—memories of badgering and memories of physical punishment that, although never severe, did little to encourage me to succeed at my schoolwork. I will say that her attitude did create in me an incredible thirst for competition, a will to come out on top, to make my parents proud of me, because, clearly, that bit of accomplishment was an anchor to their pride and self-esteem. On the other hand, her attitude probably created in me the attitude of disapproval I often found myself taking with my own children. As the Bible says, "The fathers have eaten sour grapes, and the children's teeth are set on edge" (Ezekiel 18:2).

In addition to the challenges I was facing for myself, I was also expected to be the guardian of my brother Dick while we rode the bus. One afternoon, Dick and I got separated on the bus. I was sitting at the back with my friends, and Dick was in front. Somehow, Dick became the butt of some teasing and got socked in the mouth. The bus came to a halt, the culprits were dealt with, but the damage had been done. When I got home and Mom discovered what had happened, she was furious and accused me of not looking out for my brother. I got a good thrashing, one I never forgot or forgave. My parents, especially Mom, meted out the same type of corporal punishment they had taken themselves, probably been part of the regimen at the Deaf school, as a natural part of their own parenting, and they did it with a vengeance.

For all its rustic charm, Sherry School was, for me, a tortured experience. It marked the lowest point in my life, which had been going downhill from the time of Mom and Dad's divorce, through the economic hard times, to this adolescent hell. That, however, was about to change.

7

A New Life (1951–1953)

M y education at Sherry School had lasted only that one term of the spring of 1950 because the school board had already made plans to close all the one-room schools and consolidate the students in the district into one elementary school (Grades 1–8, still no kindergarten). This new school was built just south of town on Route 111 and was initially named the Defiance Township School. Later, it was renamed the Anthony Wayne School after the local hero General Anthony Wayne, also known as Mad Anthony. The school is still active today, and my brother Art's grandson attended it at one time, but it has been expanded considerably from the little school it was when I completed the seventh and eighth grades there.

After Sherry School, this new school was luxurious. It had honest-to-God toilets, a cafeteria (no more tin lunch boxes arrayed on the wooden shelves at the back of the schoolroom), central heating, a gym with real baskets and backboards for basketball, and softball fields (baseball was banned at the new school). Now, instead of four grades in one room, we had two grades to a room, and my teacher was once again Mrs. Custer, who also acted as principal for the school. By this time, I was on my feet academically, even in math, and thrived. My parents basked in my successes and took every opportunity to attend school functions, including PTA meetings and the like, and I attended along with them to interpret. For them, everything I ever achieved was a vindication of them.

At the June 1952 eighth-grade graduation at Defiance Township School, my parents are in their Sunday best, and all four of us boys are scrubbed, necktied, and suited like the little young men we are supposed to be in America during the '50s. We are as poor as any family can be, but Mom is determined to keep us looking decent. Our little class of twenty pupils is first treated to corsages and carnations, then a sitdown dinner, and finally the ceremonies. Mom is in her element, socializing with one and all while I interpret, and Dad stands shyly by, saying nothing. I marvel at her ease, her ability to mingle with the Hearing world without a by-your-leave. She is enjoying the spotlight as the proud mother of an overachieving son and plays her role to the hilt, almost too much so to my embarrassment and, I think also, to Dad's.

After each conversation ends, the Hearing person always says, without exception, "Bob, you have such fine parents! They have done so much with what they have been given!" And then I interpret to Mom and Dad, and they smile and thank them profusely.

I think to myself, what a crock of shit! But deep down, under all the platitudes, I know they are right.

As a thirteen-year-old, I didn't have much appreciation for my parents, didn't really understand how hard their lives had been. Generally, I considered them to be fundamentally "normal" people who happened not to be able to hear. And then, when things didn't go my way, or when I saw them in a Hearing context, I perceived how different we were from each other. But as soon as I had those feelings, I was awash in guilt for what I had done; I had abandoned my parents. Most days, however, I did not think of them as "Deaf," with all the cultural implications that word has come to hold for me. My view could be stated as "Well, sure, there are some things you can't do, but other than that, you're like all my friends' parents." My parents said almost nothing about their Deafness, other than from time to time to belabor us kids with the truth that we were lucky to be able to hear or, more frequently, to talk about how lucky we were not to have gone to the Deaf school. At other times, they would use their school as a model of good education and a place in which to learn correct behavior and proper respect. We were admonished, "We were never allowed to do that at the Deaf school." It really wasn't until years later when I began reading the literature pertaining to Deafness that I had even the beginning of an understanding of who my parents were culturally and what kind of world they came from.

No matter how I viewed their Deafness, however, one aspect of our family life was clear and consistent: Money was very scarce. True, living on a subsistence family farm gave us many benefits such as ample food, free housing, and a certain security, but times were changing the general farming community. Dad and Grandpa Lloyd were running the farm on a fifty-fifty basis. For Grandpa and Grandma, their share of the small profits from the farm, when added to their Social Security benefits, provided them with a comfortable income. At the time, I never questioned this financial arrangement because it was traditional and seemed businesslike and fair, but as I look back on it as a parent who has given unstintingly to his own kids to see them through bad times, I am disturbed by how unfair it was to put business before family.

I am sure many folks in and around Defiance talked about what fine people the Newtons were to take in Richard and Elizabeth Miller, especially with Richard not even being Mr. Newton's son, and give them a job and a place to live. My grandparents were living in relative security with substantial savings in the bank while we were scraping by. My grandparents' view was that my parents were profligate, keeping up their city ways, buying all that store-bought stuff, driving miles and miles every week to visit their Deaf friends, squandering their money on gas and car expenses as well as entertainment. In fact, the money was simply not enough, and it did not compare to the incomes being enjoyed by many of their Deaf friends who had stuck it out in the city and weathered the postwar recession.

I had made a little money while I'd been staying at my grandparents' during those previous summers by raising broilers, or chickens for the table. At that time, Grandma Amy had thought it would be a good idea for me to open a savings account, and by now, I have a respectable amount in it, which becomes a thorn in my flesh and, in the end, comes near to destroying the bond between me and Mom and Dad.

Any money that goes into that account comes from me and not my grandparents, but the rule is that, once the money is in the bank, it stays there. My parents have never asked me to draw money out to help them, and in any case, I am powerless because my grandparents set the account up so two signatures are required to make withdrawals, Grandma's and

*mine. Eventually, a time comes when Mom and Dad are desperately in
need of a $90 loan, a substantial amount of money in the '50s.*

*I go to my grandparents' side of the house. Grandma is in her kitchen,
rolling out dough to make the noodles that are her signal culinary achieve-
ment in the neighborhood. Instead of slicing them in great strips, she rolls
the dough out until it is paper thin, rolls the flattened disk into a tight
cylinder, and then slices the noodles into hairlike thin strands. She explained
to me once that she began making them that way because my grandfather
Miller, who had a stomach ailment, could digest them more easily. They
rise in a heap of buttery splendor on the white floured rolling surface.*

*I begin, "Grandma, Mom and Dad are in a real pinch and they
need to borrow $90 from me. Do you think I could let them have some
money from my savings account?"*

*A long silence follows, which signals Grandma's deep disapproval. She
begins, "Well, I expect so, but I'll have to talk it over with your grandpa."
She walks into the front parlor where Grandpa is glued to the console
radio that stands next to his old armchair. I can hear him grumbling
his disapproval, although I can't make out the words.*

*She returns to the kitchen and announces, "Yes, I expect you can, but
we think you ought to have them sign a note for the money. You need to
protect yourself, or you might not get your money back."*

*I reply, "But what would be the point? I'd never be able to get my
money back just because I have a note. I couldn't call it in and I couldn't
sell it, so what's the point? And it'll just embarrass Mom and Dad."*

*She replies calmly, "Don't make any difference. You got to have a
note. You can't loan money to people without a note; that's what you got
to understand. Your grandpa and I don't feel we can go along with this
if you don't have a note."*

*I know this request will be deeply humiliating to my parents, who
are very proud people despite suffering the slights and outright abuse*

that Deaf people are subject to and, now, find themselves beholden to this smug little son of theirs.

I return to our side of the house. I explain things to my parents. As I expect, they are embarrassed, but they have no options. Mercifully, Dad draws up the note, it is signed, the money is lent and eventually repaid, and my relationship to my parents is deeply damaged.

My parents were proud of their ability to make it on their own, and they tried always to take care of their own business. For example, they requested my interpreting help only sparingly. Contrary to what seems to have been the case with many CODAs, my parents did not ask me to accompany them to doctor's appointments and the like. They set definite limits on what they thought I could and could not do, and they protected their privacy. Even now that my parents are both in their eighties, they are reluctant when my brother Art and my sister-in-law Dixie who live next door to them regularly help out with matters that require interpreting. Designing a world in which they could function independently was a serious priority for them.

Although my parents had moved sixty miles from Toledo, they managed not only to maintain their friendships with their group in Toledo but also to link up with Deaf friends all around northwestern Ohio and beyond. Deaf people tend to concentrate in urban areas where opportunities for employment are better and where a strong Deaf community already exists. To my knowledge, my parents were the only Deaf couple living in Defiance County. Keeping up their contacts with their circle of friends required regular visiting that involved a constant round of travel to and from the houses and towns as well as interminable amounts of driving. The expense was considerable, in gasoline, cars, and car repairs, and Mom's junketing, as it appeared to others, was a source of friction between my parents and my grandparents.

Grandma Amy complained constantly, and Grandpa Lloyd was always nonplussed if Dad had to go somewhere because Grandpa's notion of farming involved a seven-day-a-week, twenty-four-hour-a-day commitment to the land, the cattle, the hogs, the chickens, the sheep, the garden, and whatever. But then, if Grandpa needed any social contact, all he had to do was visit the neighbor down the road or, perhaps, make a few phone calls, although he never used the phone, letting Grandma make all the calls. He and Grandma were in constant contact with friends; people were dropping in to visit them almost daily. And, in the tradition of country hospitality that assumed that one's door was always open to company, they were always stopping to visit friends.

At first, I tended to take my grandparents' part on these issues. After all, they had control of the forum, which they expressed in my language, and I heard their side almost daily. Besides, I could see how the cost of this socializing cut into our already small income. Today, from a vantage point of years and maturity, I understand that my parents absolutely needed this activity in their lives and that my grandparents were blind to their needs. My parents were aliens in an alien culture, isolated for weeks at a time from social contact with the Deaf community. They were desperate to talk with friends of their own, much in the same way that immigrants seek out their own culture and depend on it for support, banding together in tightly knit communities.

Whenever this conflict over my parents' need to link up with their Deaf friends broke out, I was its push-pull victim. My attitude was pretty much controlled by self-interest. If the family we were visiting had kids to play with, I was ready to go. I liked visiting Deaf people. They were not dour, they did not work incessantly, they did not live frugal, stinted lives, and their kids thought and acted just like me. They joked, they laughed, and they teased. In a word, they had fun, and they were very much my people. As a CODA, I had standing in the Deaf community. I wasn't Deaf, but I was the next best thing, a CODA. This status has always stood me in good stead whenever I have been in a situation where a Deaf person needed my help, usually with interpreting. Once at my university, I came up on a maintenance crew, and the boss was trying to explain something to an electrician who was Deaf. I asked whether I could help, and then I interpreted. The electrician asked me how I knew ASL, and I signed the familiar phrase, Mother-Father Deaf, and he beamed knowingly at me. I was accepted. Much as I was immersed in Hearing culture, my home was also with my parents and the Deaf community.

Even though Dad was much more of a loner and didn't really crave the social life as much as Mom did, Mom insisted on it, especially after she went to work because work empowered her and diminished my dad's control over family decisions. She was determined to have life on her terms, finally, and she did.

Four years as the poor relation of the family finally forced Mom and Dad to come to a decision. For months, the debate had gone back and forth between them. Mom was determined to go back to work. Dad was adamantly opposed. The battles raged, and the four kids watched in awe as these two stubborn, emotional partners duked it out in ASL. In the end, Mom got her way as Dad became convinced by the simple arithmetic of our situation. In no way could we survive as a family on the farm income. Mom would go to work. Eventually, she got a job as a shirt presser in Defiance at the DeLuxe

Cleaners. At first, Dad continued the farming, and we kids took on various household chores in addition to our farm chores to make the situation work.

Mom's decision never went down well with Grandma Amy, who was of the old school, but I can't imagine how she could have proposed an alternative, given the financial bind we were in. Our farms (the main farm in Defiance County and the smaller farm in Paulding County) totaled about 140 acres, and we were milking about fourteen cows. Anyone with a sense of the economics of farming can judge that, even in the 1950s, that agricultural base could barely have supported one family, let alone two.

With milk prices spiraling downward, Dad finally had to find other work to supplement his farm income, which caused a great strain between my grandparents and us. For a long time, Grandpa Lloyd, who suffered from severe lameness in his knees, had not been able to do any work, and then, he had two serious strokes that, for a time, rendered him almost immobile. By 1953, Dad was working full-time at Johns-Manville Corporation in Defiance and farming full-time. I was being asked to bear more of the work, and the strain was beginning to show on all of us.

The farming life depended on the family's careful hoarding of resources, its making do with the goods the farm produced, and its saving cash to purchase more land. My grandparents looked backward while my parents looked ahead to the consumerist life being promoted by a burgeoning postwar economy that was bent on providing all the goods and services we had done without during the war. My parents—even my father, who was born on a farm—had not been brought up on the farm and were unacquainted with its demands. Mom and Dad had experienced strenuous upbringings but within an institutional context, at the School for the Deaf, where most of the children came from larger towns and cities and to which most of them were destined to return.

My grandfather, who was the key to upcoming changes, had no real interest in developing and adding to the farm. He had already deeded more than half of it to his wife to settle pressing debts. He had no family of his own to whom he could pass on his share. He was a childless widower, remarried late in life. Basically, the farm and Social Security provided him with an income sufficient to allow him to continue his somewhat manorial life of the past, dealing with hired men and spending most of his time hunting and fishing, which he loved passionately.

Late summer, sometime in 1952 or 1953, and the weather is hot. Grandma is canning tomatoes in her kitchen, with both the back and side doors open. A dilapidated truck pulls into the drive, carrying what appears to be a family of Mexicans or Indians on board. The driver gets out, comes to the side door, and knocks.

Grandma answers. He asks, "Excuse, we paint your roof? Aluminum paint, very cheap. We see your barn roof needs paint?" I can tell from their accent and the Oklahoma plates on the truck that they are Indians.

She replies, "Well, I'll have to get my husband to talk to you." She goes in, summons Grandpa, and brings out a large pitcher of water and a plate of molasses cookies for the woman, a teenage boy who is his dad's helper, and three children, all who are jammed into the hot cab of the truck.

Grandpa comes out onto the side stoop. "What can I do for you?"

"We seen your barn roof needs paint. We do aluminum, waterproof, last forever, very cheap. Twenty-five dollars."

He hesitates, "I don't know, that's too much for us. It's only a shed and it ain't much of a job. Do it myself for five bucks." The man looks down at Grandpa's crutches but says nothing. What Grandpa means is, I, not he, can do it, and not for five bucks but for nothing.

"We do very good job, better than brush, spray on, twenty dollars."

Grandpa waits a few minutes. "Well, I'll tell you what. I'll give you ten bucks to do it and that's my price."

I can see the look of desperation in the man's eyes. He answers, "Sir, we cannot do for ten dollars, cost that much for paint. We need gas to get to next town and have to find a job quick."

"Well, tell you what I'll do. I'll give you ten bucks and five gallons of gas, how about it?" We have a large store of gas on hand to run the farm machinery. Five gallons is worth about a dollar.

The man's look is impassive but I can sense a deep well of resentment and desperation. "Okay, sir, deal. We do it for the gas. Paint cost ten dollars."

They drive their truck out to the shed where the gasoline tank is also kept. I help them put some of the gas in the truck and some in a canister, and then they set to work.

Grandpa can't see very well, so when he looks out it appears to him that the roof is being transformed into a gleaming wonder. To me it seems a little washed out, but I say nothing. I notice a strong smell of gasoline in the air. The man and boy soon finish, collect their money, and are on their way.

Grandpa remarks, "Guess I showed them damn Messkins."

I correct him, "They weren't Mexicans, they were Indian."

He shoots back, "It's all the same"—an anthropological judgment truer than he or I realize at the time.

Two days later, it rains. Grandma and I look out at the shed from Grandma's kitchen window. The gleaming paint has begun to fade, and patches of the old rusty roof are showing through. Rivulets of aluminum liquid run down the corrugated roofing.

Grandma smiles, then says, "Oh, my!"

After the war, with the increase in agricultural mechanization, the patchwork farms soon got swallowed up by large conglomerates of farms, usually worked by one farmer on share with several landowners. With a little imagination, one can bring to life those countless thousands of mini-dramas played out by farm husbands and wives, looking over the accounts late at night at kitchen tables and tearfully deciding to pack it in. This upheaval is precisely what happened to our farm. When Dad and Grandpa Lloyd gave up farming, their enterprise was taken over by a local high-production farmer.

My grandmother, the real owner of the larger share of the farm, was so steeped in tradition and possessed of a Depression mentality that she lived to hang on to what she had. But my parents had to look to the future. They had four boys to support, and so they did what many farm families did. They found jobs in the service industry in town or in the factories. Farmers joined the assembly line, and their wives became waitresses, checkout clerks, housemaids, or shirt pressers. My parents despised the life of denial. They were the products of a new age, of television and mass advertising, and they sought the vocations that, within their limits as Deaf people, would provide the "new life" of televisions, dishwashers, dryers, store-bought clothes, and dinners out.

The tragedy of our loss of the bucolic life was not merely a tragedy of the Deaf family unable to cope with the farm; it was a tragedy of the American landscape and was, in fact, happening all around us. The farm family, surviving on the produce of the land, relying on the labor of the members of the household, possessing skills in a variety of farming enterprises such as dairying and hog or chicken raising, has now passed from the American scene and is memorialized throughout the Midwest in the ever dwindling number of all-purpose red barns and outbuildings that still survive and in the creations of writers and artists.

One afternoon in late winter 1953, Grandma Amy calls out to me as I am making my way to the house from finishing chores, "Bobby, will you tell your Dad to come on over. Grandpa's got something he needs to talk over with him."

Dad is following not far behind me, so I turn to him and tell him something is up.

We enter the little back kitchen where a nice fire in the coal stove gives the room comfortable warmth. Grandpa is sitting at the kitchen table and turns to me. He kind of mumbles, "Bob, tell your dad I've decided to sell out. We just can't manage anymore with things this way. The cows don't get the attention they need. Your dad's got more work than any of us can do. It's time to call it quits."

I turn to Dad and tell him what Grandpa has said. He doesn't react at all.

Grandpa continues, "Tell him we're keeping the farm, but I've called Yoder and Frey [the auctioneers], and we'll sell off all the machinery and stock, and your dad'll get fifty percent of everything we've bought since he came on back in '50. The same applies to the livestock. Any cows and calves that came on since '50 he'll get half, less his half of the auctioneer's commission. I'm gonna rent the farm out to John Webb. You folks can stay on in the house, and we'll work out some kind of rent. Ask him if that settlement suits him."

I explain to Dad. He simply nods, and the years of servitude come to an end. For my grandfather, it is the end of a dynasty, the end of a farming tradition that stretched back to 1863 when the Newtons first acquired the farm.

We walk out the door and around the corner to our side of the house, and Dad delivers the news to Mom, who begins immediately to plan what she will do with the money.

In 1953, the sale took place, and my parents came into a fair chunk of money, which got spent almost immediately to cover bills. Even in the best of times, my parents never were able to stick to any kind of savings plan. What came in went out. In hard times, we skimped; in good times, we splurged. It was a pattern of bingeing and starving that I have found difficult to break in my own life. My parents considered the act of saving a luxury, something you did only after you'd bought all the things you needed and had paid all your bills. What they seemed not to realize was that you never run out of needs and, most likely, will always carry some debt, no matter how much money you make.

Over the course of my adult years, I have spent more than my share of genuine angst trying to reconcile my conflicted feelings about my grandparents. Taken separately, they had their individual reasons for their share of guilt in the way they treated my parents. My grandfather had no parental feelings for my father whatever. He never treated him as a son, even a stepson. His sole interest in him was as a worker on the farm, someone he tolerated but whom, deep down, he regarded as inferior, even though my dad proved day after day that he was a bright, insightful, innovative, and clever farmer. I have often commented to my students that I believe, in his own sphere, my father was a more learned person than I with my PhD because the farm made so many demands on his thinking processes and because he had to be versed in so much lore that he needed to deal with all the problems he had to face. My grandfather had almost no respect for my father's skills and less of an inclination to place any faith in his abilities. As this disparagement became clearer to me, a rift developed between the two of us, and eventually, from about the age of fifteen on, I was barely on speaking terms with my grandfather. I think he chalked it up to teenage rebelliousness, but it went deeper than that. I hated him for what I believed he'd done to my dad and to our family. In my late age, I hold a more charitable view of him, particularly because I know he cared for me and did so much for me.

My grandmother's situation was more complex because this man, my dad, was her son. In her character, I could detect the source of my dad's shyness and his reticence, and being his son, I could also trace the source of my own. She was a well-meaning, careful, repressed woman who was steeped in misunderstanding and prejudice about Deaf people, and the fact that she had a son with whom she was barely able to communicate didn't help her overcome that prejudice. Nevertheless, in all fairness, I have to admit that my parents could be difficult and often did exhibit poor judgment. Yet, in spite of every indication my parents gave of being mature adults, Grandma Amy never could quite treat them as grown-ups. Her admiration always seemed reserved for her older Hearing son, my uncle Lester whom she loved and admired, and for his family, whom she saw as respectable, judicious, and self-reliant, whereas she maintained for us only a judgment that we were the trashy, irresponsible poor relation who always had to survive on the charity of relatives. Ironically, years later when she began to show signs of senility, her younger son (my dad) and his wife were the ones who offered to make arrangements in their lives to care for her, but they were rebuffed by Hearing relatives who felt my parents were not up to the task, and consequently, she languished in nursing homes for seven years before she died, plenty of time in which to consider the irony as best she could.

8   High School (1952–1956)

In the fall of 1952, I was bused off to an even more elegant school building, Defiance High School (now the middle school), where, for the first time in a long while, I was rubbing shoulders with kids very much like the ones I had grown up with in Toledo. As a consequence, I fared a little better than my classmates from Defiance Township School, yet I was still very much out of my element. As I mentioned earlier, my parents were still struggling financially. Buying me clothes for high school was an incredible burden for them because students were not allowed to wear jeans. So I found myself in the situation of trying to suc-ceed in a crowd of smart, affluent, middle-class town kids while my par-ents could barely afford to even have me in school. In some cases, friends of mine from the farms dropped out of school because of the cost. Every fall, my parents shouldered the burden to come up with enough money to outfit their kids for school, especially the one in high school.

In the fall of 1952, I am thrust as a freshman into the social whirl of high school. Helen Potts asks me to the Turkey Trot, the biggest social event of the fall. Helen is originally a city girl; her father bought the old George Newton farm and moved the family out to the country a short mile up the road from us toward Defiance. I have a secret crush on this gorgeous, sandy-haired, vivacious girl, but she's more a pal than a girlfriend. So far, our relationship has been all been buddy-buddy, and I suspect she's asked me out of compassion, but I don't care.

That evening, I tell Mom that Helen has asked me to the dance. Mom is ecstatic and goes into high gear; nothing propels her into action more than a social event. Because the dance is "ladies' choice," Helen pays for the tickets, which saves me some money, and I get the flowers. Dad is dragooned into doing the driving. Grandma agrees to let me take some money out of the bank to cover the flowers. Only one hitch remains: clothes.

Somehow, my parents scrape up a few dollars, and Mom and I go off on a shopping trip to Defiance, not to the fancy menswear shops such as Pixler's or Sherman's but to J. C. Penney's. There, we find the cheapest sports coat, a pair of passable trousers, and a tie, and my ultra-cheap wardrobe is complete. Luckily, I have a decent pair of shoes that will pass.

At the dance, everything is too weird. Helen is way out of my league. She moves in another world at school, and I sense from the way her friends react to me that I am a real bumpkin in this crowd, with my home-cut hair and my ill-fitting coat with cuffs that hang down to my knuckles and rear flap that rides up unflatteringly on my butt. But Helen's a good sport, doesn't lose her poise, and we have a good time. We end the evening at a party at Carolyn Ingle's, where we all try to pass out by hyperventilating into a paper bag—hot times for fourteen-year-olds!

When Dad brings me home, Mom is waiting. She says, "Bobby, now you have a girlfriend, this is a good thing for you. Helen is a wonderful girl!"

I reply, "Sure, Mom." Then I go upstairs. How can they understand? How can I explain it to them, who I really am—just the kid of Deaf parents who's lucky even to get a foot in the door.

My mother's romantic aspirations for me were so wide of the mark that I didn't even bother to try to make her understand what kind of a place Defiance High School was, with its glitzy girls in expensive poodle skirts, who exuded health and wealth, and their male counterparts in their convertibles, their "hot cars," who displayed their immaculate smiles and their tanned, muscled bodies. I wasn't alone, but I and others who were not in that exclusive group lived in a world apart.

Defiance in the '50s was a much different place from the Defiance we had left in 1942. After World War II, it changed dramatically when the General Motors Corporation built its central foundry plant just east of the city limits, and the town was catapulted from a rather sleepy burg into a small industrial city. Yet in spite of the company's many contributions to Defiance, I have always resented the fact that GM would never hire my dad because of his deafness, even though he had had three years of experience working the assembly line at Willys-Overland during the war and was a UAW member in good standing.

General Motors was soon joined by the Johns-Manville Corporation, which took over an old factory facility near downtown, expanded it, and converted the pleasant downtown area into a stench-laden, industrial ghetto that the local citizenry had to tolerate because of the jobs J-M provided. Later, the company added a new facility just outside town. My father, as I said, held one of those J-M jobs, as did my brother John.

As my parents made the change from home to work and from farm to factory, our financial circumstances eased, and I managed to fit in better. I was proud of my parents, no matter how conflicted my private feelings were. I never felt any shame attached to being with them or signing to them in public. Yet disappointment came with having to hear the remarks of people around me, especially when they assumed that I, too, couldn't hear. I had grown up with the impolite stares of strangers, as had my parents. We just rattled on, oblivious to the attention we got. It was part of the package as far as I was concerned.

Still, as I struggled with the incredible disparity between the poverty of my life and the comfortable lives of my friends, I was constantly humbled and guilty because I was embarrassed by my situation. By day, I was expected to be the bright, successful, ambitious young high schooler every small-town parent admires. After school, I faced the truth of my life: parents who, to much of the world around me, appeared freakish and strange and a home life that made my school life a sham.

In fact, my parents fit in much better in the rural environment, among farmers and blue-collar workers, than they did in town society. In a small town short on news, a common custom is to run stories about academic achievements at the high school, so from time to time, I managed to make it into print for being on the honor roll or for receiving some special award. If a ceremony was involved, my parents would dutifully attend, and I would continue my task of interpreting. High school affairs, however, were lavish, and often, my poor parents found themselves smack up against any number of middle-class, educated couples who were unfailingly polite but also somehow stunned to discover that this bright boy was the son of Deaf parents.

One trick I had learned long ago was to broadcast as far and as often as possible that I had Deaf parents, so we would all be spared the embarrassment of a surprise. Still, we had to contend with those unanticipated moments when some adult, usually a teacher to whom I was too shy to talk, would speak to Mom or Dad before I could get out an alert. "So nice to see you, Mr. and Mrs. Miller. We're very proud of Bob's accomplishments here." Mom and Dad smile apologetically while I quickly explain, "My mom and dad are Deaf. I'll have to interpret for you," which I do while the Hearing person makes an effort at a recovery.

Frank Blue, my algebra teacher as well as the assistant principal and disciplinarian for the school, strikes such fear in me that I cannot recite in his class without forcing myself to open my mouth. I am not alone. Because I'm such a speck on the wallpaper, Blue is convinced that I'm an average student, so I manage to pull the usual average grades until the state algebra test is given and I score second in my class of 160 students. At first, he refuses to believe I've done that well. Then, when he finds out from another teacher that my parents are Deaf, he is dumfounded. Shortly after, he takes me aside in the hall and says to me, "Bob, that's good work you are doing. I hear your parents are Deaf. They must be very proud of you." From then on, nothing but As in algebra.

As a teenager and the firstborn, not only was I called on to do more than my share of interpreting but also was required to take on the onerous task to introduce my parents to the traditions of teen culture because they had never really had a chance to be teenagers, never really experienced what it meant. Although my parents retain affectionate recollections of their years at the School for the Deaf, I have bitter feelings about their experience. I resent the institution that did such a poor job teaching them and preparing them for the realities of life. Dating, borrowing the car, asserting one's independence, and just generally being a teenager were experiences that were foreign to them. Many battles were waged in the Miller household between teenage son and mystified parents as we strove to accommodate each other during those years of growing up. True to the American teenage code, I was rebellious, I was misunderstood, and I had a smart mouth and the rage to go with it. Along with my peers, I was also a member of the first real teenage postwar generation, obsessed with the music of Elvis Presley and the movies of James Dean. I had parents who were "out of it," Deaf parents who I thought were from Mars when it came to understanding my life. I was the quintessential victim.

My mother's expectations for her kids were often completely unrealistic, and to an extent, I was to blame, or at least, I felt a huge burden of guilt for the pressure she brought on my brothers because she expected them all to excel as I had excelled. Although they did well, they did not do well enough in her eyes. In John's case, it became clear that he was slightly learning disabled, probably as a result of birth trauma, and would never be able to learn at the pace the rest of us set. To his credit, he graduated from high school, served ably in the Army, and lived a full and useful life until his death in 2002.

It is the summer of 1953. I am fourteen, have just finished my first year in Defiance High School, and am anticipating another good year come fall. Mom has given me the task of teaching my youngest brother

Johnny the alphabet. I taught it to Artie a couple of years earlier at Mom's insistence because she has fixed in her mind the conviction that every kid has to know the alphabet before he or she enters first grade. Teaching it to Artie had been a breeze. Johnny, however, has difficulty getting the hang of it. "Okay, John, let's go now—A, B, C."

"A, B, C."

"D, E, F."

"D, E, F."

"G, H, I."

"G, H, I."

"Now put them together for me."

Johnny begins hesitantly, "A, B, C . . ."

"Go on, Johnny, you can do it!" I begin to lose patience.

"I can't 'member."

I lose it completely. We've been at it for a half hour and have been getting nowhere. "Jesus, John, there's nothing to it—ABC, DEF, GHI— just like that!"

"I can't 'member."

We call it quits. Later, I try to explain to Mom, "Johnny just can't pick it up that easy. It's too hard for him to just memorize the letters. It doesn't mean anything to him."

She gets upset. "He has to learn it. He has to be ready for school."

I explain again, "I don't think he can do it. He has a hard time. I don't think it really matters if he knows it or not."

She does not relent, "He MUST learn it. Teacher will think he is a stupid boy. You are not doing it right, like with Artie. You do it right, teach him the right way, not lie to me!"

Somehow, by the end of the summer, Johnny learns the alphabet, but it really means nothing to him, and the cost in screaming has been too much for either of us.

I announce to Mom, "Johnny knows the alphabet now."

She beams and replies, "That's good. Now he will be a smart boy in school."

I don't know how to explain it to her, so I say nothing.

I had learned to drive at eleven, as soon as I'd moved onto the farm, because I was needed to run tractors and drive vehicles to fields to carry lunch and beverages as well as deliver tools and the like to my dad. Ordinarily, my driving was limited to the tractors, but from time to time, I got to drive trucks and cars, mostly in the fields, and once in a while, I had to venture onto the road, State Route 111, a busy and dangerous highway. Like all my friends, by the time I had reached legal driving age, I was already an accomplished driver.

Grandpa Lloyd was more progressive about the driving issue than Dad, but it was out of necessity because he was such a terrible driver. During my preteen years, I served as Grandpa Lloyd's "driving guide" as we careened down rural two-lane roads in search of new fishing spots or ponds where we would seine for crawfish, the best bait for sheephead. He would casually wander from lane to lane in his 1936 Plymouth two-door sedan, barely able to see through his tobacco-juice-splattered eyeglasses. My most memorable trip with him was to Defiance one summer morning to pick up his new eyeglasses (he had dropped his old ones over the side of the boat), and my job was to hang out the passenger window and warn this man, now driving with no glasses at all, if he got onto the berm. As the months passed and his driving became more and more erratic, he often just piped up, "You wanna drive?" I'd say, "Sure," and off we'd go. I would be illegal as hell, but he didn't care. To me, that was cool.

The day I turned sixteen, I presented myself to Dad as ready to be a licensed driver. At the time, I think the waiting period between issuance of a permit and applying for a license was one week. So I got the permit, and a week later, I went with Dad to take the test. He was sure I would fail; otherwise, I don't think he'd have let me take the test. I passed. No farm kid ever failed the driving test. To have done so would have meant dishonor to the code of the farm kid. Then began the usual battle between parents and son over use of the car, an American ritual of the times, especially in a family that could barely afford to keep one car. The battle became bloodier because my parents were totally mystified by my need for wheels.

Even more agonizing for them was dating, a social custom completely foreign to my parents. Fortunately, my dating life was practically nonexistent because I didn't have the money to support it and because, as a CODA, I was stigmatized as "that boy with those Deaf parents," genetically suspect, and therefore not prime dating material.

Dating in small-town Ohio in the '50s was a serious business. In my case, the usual scenario went something like this progression. I ask a girl out. She consents. Her parents find out my parents are Deaf. The girls makes a hurried phone call, and the date's off. Or, she goes out, we have a great time, her parents find out about my parents, and that's the end. I found the whole routine puzzling and was never able to make real sense of it until some years after the fact when, in my reading, I discovered that this experience is common among CODAs.

In some social classes like mine (definitely lower), dating was considered as serious courtship leading directly to marriage, and who wanted their daughter dating a kid that might produce deaf children? When I did manage to get a date, the event was greeted by my parents with elation and fear—elation because I was being accepted, which meant a great deal to Mom, who wanted us to have the social life she never had, and fear because I was an oversexed product of the '50s who was out alone in a car in the company of a girl, fear that was justified.

Dating meant sex, and again, my parents were at sea when it came to dealing with the issue. In our family, sex was never talked about in any way, and my parents had severely puritanical attitudes on the subject, attitudes that had been inculcated in them by their families, by a culture that feared what might come of intermarriage among Deaf people, and by a harshly repressive institutional training that was determined to prevent the occurrence of any kind of "unfortunate" sexual behavior in the school. Besides, as I like to describe myself during these years, I was the Great Deaf Hope, and my mother, partly from her own experience and partly from fear, dreaded the possibility that I would carelessly fall into an early marriage that would ruin my life. Given the state of contraceptive methods at that time, she was right to be afraid. To a boy who grew up in the '50s, the condom display in any drugstore in the '90s still is a wonder to behold.

Sex was an anathema, and masturbation, its evil twin, was almost as bad if not worse. When it became apparent through my own carelessness that I was "abusing" myself, Dad gave me a lecture on how, if I continued doing "it," I would go mad. At the time, I also had a case of acne, and Mom and Dad took this as evidence that I was hopelessly caught in "the habit." Dad referred to talks he had been given in classes at the Deaf school. I kept thinking, "That goddamned school!"

To help me reform myself, he gave me a sex manual replete with line drawings of male and female genitalia, none of which I could recognize, particularly the female equipment, and a detailed account of "the act." After all, ours was a family of all males but one, and I had never seen a naked adult female in the flesh and could remember only some vague details from Jimmy Stone's descriptions of his mother back in Toledo. Equally vague were my memories of pornographic comics ("eight-pagers" or "Tijuana bibles") that got passed around at school until they were falling apart and of my brother's and my accidental intrusions into the bathroom in the apartment while my mother was bathing. Those were guaranteed to bring shrieks from Mom, which, at first, threw me into complete panic but, later, got turned into a hilarious mime that Dick and I used to act out. Later, Dick and I and the Schatz boys supplemented our sketchy information with a cache of nudist-camp magazines we found hidden away in our parents' bedroom, but that sexual paradise soon fell when, one night, Dad discovered us in bed under our blankets with flashlights, the naughty magazines spread out around us.

Somehow, we all got through the ordeal of being a teenager and parents of a teenager. As the oldest, I managed to introduce Mom and Dad to the folkways of teen life and, I think, paved the way for my three brothers, who I hope are grateful for what I did for them. Although I may have had a tougher time of it because my parents were so innocent about booze, sex, and rock and roll (drugs came later but I was away at school by then and free to indulge in "reefer madness" on my own), I think they treated me remarkably kindly, more kindly in some ways than the parents of my Hearing friends treated their kids. Some of what I thought at the time were problems created by my parents were actually a sign of changing times in America itself, and the difficulties I was having were not unique to me. Besides, I shamefully admit as I have before, that, because my parents were Deaf and somewhat naïve, they were all the easier to deceive, and deceive them I did—at least, most of the time.

I decide to sneak out of the house for a late-night rendezvous with some of my high school buddies. They're depending on me because I have the wheels. I've made these escapades often and have worked out a routine.

Even though my parents are deaf, I use extra caution sneaking past their open bedroom door because they are extremely sensitive to vibrations, and any creaking of the floor or stair steps will wake them up. One of the old floorboards emits a huge groan, but luckily no one wakes up—or so I think.

Outside, in the dark of the garage, I unhook the odometer, which I have learned to do because Dad has made a practice of recording the mileage. Then, off I go to Defiance. I pick up my friends, and we head for another buddy's place where we get high on some Vat 69 Scotch, foul stuff that makes me so sick I never want to see it again. In spite of my state of drunkenness, I manage to get home, into the garage, up the stairs, and into bed beside my brother Art, who doesn't suspect I've been gone.

In the morning, a Sunday, I manage to get downstairs and perform my libations before anyone else is up. Dad comes ambling down the stairs, walks out the kitchen door, and proceeds out to the garage. I break out in a sweat.

He comes back in. "Where were you with the car last night?"

I wheedle, "What? What do you mean?"

He grabs me by the arm, and I follow because Dad is super-strong and hasn't lost any of his youthful athleticism. He pulls me out to the garage. "There, what do you see?"

I look around, say smartly, "How should I know? I see the car, OK?"

He points to the back of the car, "Tire tracks. Those are tire tracks. You had the car out last night because I brushed out all the tire tracks when I put it in the garage. You know what?"

Yes, I know what. I'm grounded.

Dad was clever. Tire tracks leading out of the garage and back in, odometers disconnected, hidden bottles of liquor—nothing got by Dad. He dedicated himself to catching out his devious sons and usually succeeded.

With Mom and Dad both working, our lives began to take on some stability. We had been teetering on the edge of financial disaster ever since Dad lost his job with Willys-Overland in 1945, but by the close of 1953, our situation had become tolerable, even comfortable. Nevertheless, even with two stable incomes and a rent rate that was minimal (thanks to Grandma Amy), my parents never could seem to hold onto money. It has eluded them all their lives. Of course, we had the standard expenses, but to those obligations, my parents would add the costs of another car, fancy clothes for Mom and clothes she bought for Dad, gadgets that somehow seemed to soak up whatever extra cash my parents had, and unwise financial decisions that, once again, proved how unprepared their education had rendered them for the world of work and family.

As soon as I was of legal age, I got part-time work with the local movie theater firm and then, a bit later, transferred to my mom's place of employment, DeLuxe Dry Cleaners. My job was to sort and wash clothes and then re-sort and package the washed shirts. When things were slow, I'd do janitorial chores. This move put us cheek by jowl once again and brought to the fore all the problems that went with it. In some ways, I liked the association with Mom because I had worked alongside Dad for those years on the farm and had benefited in many ways from the close contact, which most kids today do not receive from their parents. Mom was a first-rate shirt presser, the best in town, and she brought in much more business than the dry cleaners could handle (and more business than she was fairly compensated for). In other ways, our working together heightened the conflict between us.

I was the conduit through which the bosses funneled criticism to my mother. I was the interpreter once again who had to take responsibility for misunderstandings on both sides. The flip side of the arrangement was that my mother became the conduit to me of criticism of my work from both bosses and workers, and she lived in dread that I would be sacked from the only available job in town, one that I had to have to keep afloat in high school.

The business was a partnership between Paul Kerr and the Reverend Joseph Coleman Richards, D.D., formerly pastor of the local Methodist church, who had lost his post for refusing to accept a transfer to another parish. The whole matter ended up in court where Richards's cause did not prevail, and shortly thereafter, he surfaced as co-owner of the dry cleaning enterprise. His daughter Judy (later Judy Hope) was, for a time, a classmate of my brother Dick and of my future wife, and she was a good friend. She later went to Wellesley and Harvard Law and then on to a distinguished career in the Ford administration and in the law.

Joe Richards was a colorful figure with a flair for showmanship. Among his parishioners, he had inspired either undying loyalty and admiration or bitter hatred. He insisted on being called "Doctor" Richards in deference to his Doctor of Divinity degree and generally encouraged a personality cult to grow up around him. While he had been a pastor, he had always worn a doctoral robe for church services. One of his special prides was his marvelous tenor voice, and for every Sunday service, he had reserved the singing of the opening solo, "This Holy Hour," to himself. He was the most gifted homilist I have ever heard preach. He had a remarkable memory, a quick mind, a stentorian speaking voice, and a genuine flair for the rhetorical that would have been admired by the great Roman orator Cicero himself. His wife, Eve, was a role model for all of us, beautifully

mannered, cultured, but very down to earth. When we got behind
on orders, she pitched in and took her turn at the presses, and she
was damned good at it. Needless to say, Joe did not do any pressing,
and we were relieved that he didn't.

*Paul Kerr, one of the owners, comes chirping down the ramp from the
lobby into the plant area. He turns to me with a rather sly, ironic look, and
in his most honeyed tone, announces to me, "Oh, Bob! I need to have you
ask your mother to pay more attention to the way she's doing collars.
We're getting so many complaints!"*

*I sign to Mom, "Paul says the customers are complaining about the
way you're doing the collars."*

*Mom gets that perturbed look on her face, and replies, "Ask him
what's wrong with them."*

*Which I do, and he responds, "Tell Elizabeth there are just too many
wrinkles and puckers, and if she can't do it better, we'll have to do something about it. We just can't have bad quality work going out of the shop
like that. Would you tell her that, in a nice way, would you? Thank you,
Bob." He heels away and heads over to the washer.*

*As diplomatically as I can, I explain to Mom. She gets the message and
tears well up in her eyes, as much from the experience of being humiliated in front of her son as from the threat to her job.*

The relationship between Richards and Kerr was always a tense one.
Finally, it came to an end, and I assume that Paul was bought out,
making Richards sole owner of the business. Richards knew little

about the nuts and bolts of dry cleaning, even though he was a good businessman. He constantly insisted on meddling in the working end of the business, to the detriment of everyone's efforts. Although he had been a great preacher, he was not a skillful laborer in the vineyard of dry cleaning, and his determination to put in a hand usually had dire and highly comical results. He lost shirts with alarming regularity. On one occasion, in a hurry to load the washer, he forgot to check all the shirt pockets, and a load of fifty shirts got sliced up by a razor blade that someone had forgotten to take out of his pocket. On another occasion, he missed a ballpoint pen and wound up with a load of pretty blue shirts. In his hurry to move the work along, he was constantly opening the door of the huge front-loading washer to pop in another shirt, consequently flooding the laundry area with gallons of hot water and sopping shirts.

After a time, dealing with Richards got to be an annoyance, and besides, the pay was pitiful, so I searched around for another job and found one selling shoes at the Villa Shoe Store, a more lucrative and less strenuous occupation and one I turned out to be good at. And I stayed with it until I left for college. Mom outlasted Richards and remained with DeLuxe through several changes of ownership until her retirement. And every owner recognized what an asset she was.

Grandpa has had a serious stroke and is now on crutches, and he's had to give up fishing. It's a cool June morning in 1955, and I have the bug to try our favorite spot on Six Mile Creek—something I hardly ever do— and, like the lazy kid I am, I don't push off until about ten o'clock. To Grandpa, that is the worst sin of all. Anyone knows you don't catch fish if you don't get up early. I ask if I can borrow the boat. He leans on his

crutches in the back doorway and calls out all kinds of discouragement. "Won't catch 'em this time of day. I see you got old bait—won't get anything on that stuff. Anyway, it's too late. They've shut the dam down." But he lets me have the boat.

And we both know. We know.

I get back about three-thirty, walk up into the yard with a stringer of six hefty sheephead, all more than three pounds, as fine a stringer as he's ever seen.

He comes out, barely able to move on his crutches. He looks at the fish, then me. He tries to blink away the tears, but can't, and I watch them roll down his cheeks into the stubble that peppers his jowls. Then he turns and shuffles away. We both know he will never go fishing again. And for a long time, neither will I.

In the fall of 1955, I became a senior, and suddenly, after I'd had only passing success with girls and had dated only occasionally when I could afford it, I met a gorgeous, dark-haired, bright-eyed girl from the little town of Evansport and fell in love. In later years, I kidded her that I had to go out of town to find a girl whose parents hadn't tumbled to the truth about my parents and me. The whole thing was a little crazy, and yet in so many ways, we turned out to be right for each other. We were both bright kids from impoverished but proud families. We both had our struggles, inside our families and outside them. We were young, and we were immature, but why argue with forty-plus years of successful marriage? Socially and culturally, we were more closely matched than we realized. In our own ways, we were both hardworking and ambitious—and desperate to break out of the lives we'd been leading.

Dick, John, Art, Bob, in the kitchen at the farm, on John's birthday, January 1955.

My mother was alternately delighted and horrified that I was involved with a girl. Her rather naïve ambitions for my social success now came up against a harsh reality. What would happen to my plans to go to college? What if Diane got pregnant? Mom reacted as if I had been headed for the priesthood. The resulting conflicts left their mark on relations between my future wife and her mother-in-law-to-be, but over the years, Diane has become a treasure to my mother.

Sometime in late winter of 1956, I bring home my grade cards from school—three Bs and two As—a fall from grace for me. Mom is furious. She begins screaming at me, signing, "Why you spend so much time with that girl, you are a silly boy, all you think of is girl, girl!" She demands that I break up with Diane. Reluctantly, I agree. The next

night, on the Partees's front porch after a movie date, I ask Diane for my ring back. Tearfully, she gives it to me, but we agree to keep seeing each other. That night I realize I can't overcome my mother's control over me and that I am truly my father's son.

My last year of high school was a success that was celebrated by my parents and me. I was elected class president. I graduated with high honors. I got high scores on my entrance exams and had my pick of schools, although my finances set me on a course for Bowling Green State University, about fifty miles away. Bowling Green had made the decision all the more attractive by offering me a full scholarship, which I kept throughout my undergraduate years there.

My family had always understood that I would be going to college. Back in the seventh grade, Mrs. Custer had asked each of us in class what our plans were, and I'd replied that I would be a farmer like my father. This encounter occurred in 1951, before my father had decided to leave off farming completely. Mrs. Custer looked at me and said, "Well, there's no way you'll be a farmer. You'll understand what I mean soon enough." Experiences like that tended to give me a big head, and down the road, I would discover that, talented as I may have been, others were around who were more talented than I. It took me some time to get an accurate measure of my abilities. But in high school, I did thrive, and I made many friends.

On May 25, 1956, just before I was to graduate, Grandpa Lloyd died at the age of seventy-six, leaving Grandma Amy a widow for the third time in her life and the sole owner of the farm. His wish was that whatever I needed for college should be given me, and Grandma made good on his promise. Costs not covered by either my summer savings or my scholarship Grandma took care of, willingly. With Grandpa's death, an important period in my life was concluding. It had actually come to a close with the breakup of the partnership between Grandpa and Dad back in 1953, but now two events, Grandpa's death and my upcoming departure for college, were bringing this stage of my life to an end. But first, I would be subjected to one more uncomfortable family situation.

After years of living smack up against her in-laws, my mother thinks she has figured out a way to finance a home, and Grandma, now the sole owner of the farm and living quite comfortably on the farm income and her Social Security check, with substantial savings in the bank, easily has the wherewithal to make this dream come true. Grandma has also made it public that her estate will be divided equally between her two sons, Dad and Uncle Lester. The decision to allow both her sons to share equally in the inheritance is Solomonic; the decision to make it public turns out to be a mistake.

Almost immediately, Mom prods Dad and me to ask Grandma to deed them some land, which they can then use as collateral for a down payment (using the land as equity) on a new house. I am given the job of asking, which I try to get out of doing.

I walk out the kitchen door and around to Grandma's kitchen door. Grandpa has been dead for some weeks now.

I open by saying, "Grandma, Mom and Dad wanted me to ask you if you'd be willing to give them a little land at the corner of the pasture so they can use it as collateral for a loan. Then they could get started on building that house they want."

Grandma stands in the kitchen, looks out the window for a minute or two, then turns to me and says, "I'll think about it." I go back around into our kitchen and deliver the message, which means, "Never."

In desperation, Mom decides to take matters into her own hands, which means something is going to turn out badly. She says we will go talk to Grandma's attorney, Karl Weaner, and ask him how she and Dad might be able to draw on their interest in Grandma's estate.

I tell her, "He's not going to tell you anything. He'll think you are a fool. He'll think you are trying to do something crooked." Dad is uncomfortable with the plan, but he gives in. I am drafted to do the interpreting.

The appointment is made, the three of us appear and sit down in Mr. Weaner's conservatively decorated office. I begin by explaining the situation, and as I do, Mr. Weaner's face turns to stone. (It is stony in any case, only it gets stonier.)

I say, "Mom and Dad understood that Grandma's will names Dad and his brother as sole heirs?"

PAUSE.

Weaner replies, "I am not at liberty to say."

I continue, "If Dad is named as a beneficiary in the will, is there any way they can draw on those assets in anticipation of his inheritance?" (God, did I ever know the answer to that one!)

PAUSE.

"I am not at liberty to say."

I continue, "Is there any way at all that Mom and Dad can draw on these assets?"

PAUSE.

"Yes, there is. Ask Mrs. Newton if she will lend or give your parents the money for the down payment on the house."

End of conference. Needless to say, I soften the tone of the conversation for my parents' sake.

Out in the car, Mom breaks into tears. She is bitterly disappointed but also angry because, once again, her smart-ass son has been right.

In their effort to find some way to convince Grandma to give them a start, my parents made an incalculable mistake and suffered the ultimate humiliation, to crawl behind Grandma's back and then be rebuffed. After the years of commitment to the farm, to my grandparents, and then to my grandmother, my parents, who were now in their forties and who had survived so much, were still being treated in a paternalistic, infantile way. Even though Grandma Amy had spent years of living and dealing with Mom and Dad, she was unable to break through the fear and anxiety and make a commitment of trust and, yes, of love. But nothing could be done about that. What a sad thing, for a mother not to have faith in her son. Dad, as usual, didn't say a word. For me it was "déjà vu all over again." The episode was soon forgotten, and I think Mr. Weaner understood the situation better than he let on and kept his counsel in the matter.

Finally, on a long-awaited warm September day in 1956, I stood in my dorm room in Rodgers Quad, on the campus of BGSU as we called it, introducing myself and my proud parents to my roommates. I was the first person from either side of my family to go to college. I was also about to have a bed of my own for the first time since I'd slept in a crib. My life with my parents and brothers had come to an end. From that time forward, I visited home often, but I had little knowledge of what was going on there unless it happened to press in on my life, which was rarely.

The scales were lifted from my eyes during those college terms and on into graduate school. After all those years on the farm, years sheltered in a small-town school where the American verities were honored day in and day out, I was ready for the "shock of the new" that came from my history, literature, science, and philosophy courses, and I became even more jaded in my attitude toward my parents. Nevertheless, I never lost my respect for them, my appreciation of their struggles. I knew, however, that we inhabited vastly different worlds, so I kept my ties strong but simple as we struggled along in our primitive conversations in ASL. On the one hand, I could not believe that they could even begin to comprehend what was happening to me, and they did not. On the other hand, they tolerated my simplistic conversations with them as I struggled with a language that I seldom used and then only when I conversed with them. Yet somehow the tie held, and we kept coming back to each other, through grandchildren and, eventually, great grandchildren, so somehow, we never forgot what we had been through, and how we had survived it.

9

Closure (1999–2002)

*I*n *1999, on a brisk, late-winter day in northwestern Ohio, Diane and I drive my mother, who is now eighty-one, to see her younger two sisters, Eleanor and Dorothy. Both sisters are in a nursing home just outside Upper Sandusky. Dad has begged off traveling today. Mom had hoped her youngest sister, Jean, who lives in Fostoria, could make it so all the sisters could be there together, but she has a bad cold. My cousin Sharyn, Eleanor's oldest daughter, now retired from her speech and drama teaching position at the local high school, has become guardian of the two senile women, both of whom are widowed. That act is of special value to Dorothy, who is childless.*

We arrive at Eleanor's room to find her neatly dressed in an attractive running suit, reclining, watching TV. She smiles at us but does not recognize anyone.

Mom, ever the social butterfly, is determined to have a kind of reunion of her and her sisters and goes looking for Dorothy. She finds her in her room in her wheelchair and still in her pajamas. We summon a cheery nurse and ask whether Dorothy can be dressed for a visit, and she readily complies. We return to Eleanor's room, but we can hear Dorothy down the hall, her hoarse deaf vocalizations, yelling a mighty resistance to being prepared for her visitors.

Finally, she is wheeled in. Her hair is still a mess; she tries to curl up into a fetal position and refuses to acknowledge my mother. Last year, she lost the ability to sign, and her communication now is limited to pitiful cries for "Momma."

Mom attempts to communicate, but Dorothy turns her head away from her, then lunges forward at her. Eleanor is getting visibly upset, so we call for the nurse to wheel Dorothy back to her room. Mom gives Eleanor a kiss, and we make our way out through the front entrance.

In the car, Mom turns to me briefly and gestures, a convention that Deaf people use to signal the beginning of a conversation. She is on the verge of telling me something, then changes her mind, shakes her head, and looks off into the distance at the dead, broken cornstalks and drifted snow.

Defiance has developed into a typical growth-oriented, boosterish, midwestern small city of more than 20,000 inhabitants, with the usual dying downtown area, filled with craft shops and a martial arts parlor. What was a charming shopping area shows the beginnings of seediness and decay. It has been replaced on the north side of town by a conglomerate of mall and franchise stores, an area where you can visit with neighbors or power walk within the comfortable confines of the Northtowne Mall, shop at K-mart or Meijer's, and eat at McDonald's, Pizza Hut, or Bob Evans.

Dad continued to work at Johns-Manville until his retirement in 1982, as did my brother John until he took permanent disability in 1998. My brother Art worked at GM until his early retirement in 1996. Like me, my brother Dick shook the dust of Defiance from his feet. Dick had a twenty-year military career after which he went on to earn a college degree and taught industrial arts in Birmingham, Alabama, for the Veterans Administration. He is now fully retired and lives in Illinois. Professor Bob, as I am affectionately known, also went on to earn not only a college degree but also graduate degrees and is the only Miller son still working.

The factories in Defiance still operate today in their same locations, although Johns-Manville expanded into another plant outside town, and its downtown plant no longer emits noxious gases, thanks to EPA requirements. GM, now called GM Powertrain, is still the major employer in the area, although rumors circulate from time to time around town that GM is planning to shut down the outmoded plant. I continue to resent GM because it denied employment to my dad. At one point, the plant required workers driving foreign cars to park in a special area, but soon after that, it began turning out engine blocks for Toyota, and the parking-lot ghetto disappeared almost overnight. Rumors of closing keep Defiance citizens living on the edge and continually expecting economic Armageddon.

Grandma Amy lived on at the farm on her side of the house until 1966, squirreling away her money and daily showing disturbing signs of senility. The defining moment came when a man broke into her home and tried to rob her, or so she said. She was shaken but proud that he hadn't gotten a dime from her as she fought him off. She confided that she'd been carrying a considerable amount of cash pinned inside her dress. This episode, along with other minor disasters, prompted Uncle Lester, Dad's brother, to decide to place her in a nursing home. My parents were reluctant, but once again, the

Hearing world prevailed. For the first few years of her stay, she was relatively normal though a little forgetful, but gradually, she succumbed to the full effects of senility and institutionalization. She survived at the home for seven long years, until 1973—a depressing, miserable end to a difficult life in which she had endured the deaths of a child and three husbands as well as her youngest child's loss of his hearing. My last view of her was of a small, wizened woman of about sixty pounds, bedridden, shrunken into a fetal position, and totally lost to the world around her. After she died, we discovered a cache of old broken toys and a couple of my softballs from more than twenty years ago, which she had hidden in a back corner of a closet, the Rosebuds of her former life at home with her grandsons.

It is June 4, 1973, a Monday, the day of Grandma Amy's funeral and the day before Diane's and my thirteenth wedding anniversary. As we prepare to drive to the funeral home in Oakwood, the family gathers at the farmhouse where my parents still live. This occasion is the first time my brothers and I have all been together in several years. John is back from his army service in Korea, and Dick and Art have both returned safely from their tours of duty in Vietnam. Because of my blind eye and my age, I am the only brother to be passed up by the military. I am deeply anti-war, but discreetly avoid the topic. Diane and I have driven up from Louisville where I am now an associate professor at the university.

Grandma is laid out in a billowy peach-colored bit of chiffon, quite out of keeping with her preference for plain garments. Several people comment on the skill of the undertaker, "She looks just like she did twenty years ago, just like she's sleeping." She does looks more like herself than she did in those last years at the nursing home. Uncle Will Miller, Grandma's brother-in-law, has come from Bellevue, driven over by his daughter and Dad's cousin Betty Burson. He is still hale at the age of ninety-two and will live on for almost six more years. I wonder how he has lived so long when his brother Henry, my grandfather, died in his forties.

Mom asks me whether I will interpret for her, Dad, Aunt Dorothy, and Uncle Warren, and I agree. I sit on a wooden chair next to Reverend Eichenauer of the Junction Bible Christian (formerly Methodist) Church, a pleasant man, but unfortunately, he knows nothing about my grandmother and keeps asking me for bits of information about her.

As I begin to interpret, I realize that I have forgotten the signs for Christ and God and holy and the other host of religious words I used to know, but gradually, they come back to me. As I sign, I notice that not only my parents and my aunt and uncle but also everyone else is watching me instead of the preacher. I begin to realize that, through signing, his clichéd utterances take on an eloquence they do not have in the vocalized world and that, somehow, the gestures give a spiritual meaning to the voicings, as if I am speaking in tongues through my hands to a Hearing world that can truly understand me. How ironic it is, Grandma, that you are celebrated in death by a language you could never come to terms with in life.

Grandma is buried in the Junction Cemetery, next to her husband Henry, my father's father, under the cedar tree he wanted planted over his grave so he could lie in the shade. Nearby is their infant daughter, Hilda, and not far off are Grandma's parents, three of her sisters and two brothers, and a host of relatives and friends. Diagonally across the cemetery are my great grandparents Adam and Frances Miller and two of their daughters, great aunts Emma Levy and Sarah Angela Miller.

Grandma is home now, "Daheim ist's gut, home 'tis well."

Dad and Uncle Lester sold the Newton farm to John Webb, and Mom and Dad built their new house on a five-acre parcel of the farm where they live today. In spite of my efforts to convince them to finance their new home, my parents chose to pay for it up front, and then gradually, the remainder of Dad's inheritance got spent for furnishings for the new home, a new car, settlement of bills until, eventually, nothing was left. But Mom had her home at last. The Other Place had been sold earlier to Dad's cousin, Ralph Miller, and the old house that I have so many happy memories of was destroyed in a brush fire that reportedly got out of control. Nothing remains there but open field.

My parents have lived to see me complete my education, marry, raise three daughters, become a professor, a grandfather, and move toward the close of a successful career. My relationship with Mom and Dad improved and strengthened throughout the many years that followed my leaving home in 1956 during which I finished my graduate work and established myself in my academic calling, although I think they were disappointed that I didn't become a doctor or lawyer or the CEO of a major corporation. Somehow or other, they have now convinced themselves that I am wealthy, and brag to friends that I am "rich," which I suppose I am by their standards.

For all the maturity that was expected of me during my adolescence, I left home in 1956 still a willful, stubborn child. Gradually, I acquired what I lacked, a perspective and an understanding of my parents and their Deaf world, partly through my own reading and partly through the wisdom that we all hope will come with growing older.

My mother, who yearned for a daughter all her married life and never had one, became deeply attached to our three girls, all of whom are now adults, two with families of their own. My daughters, unlike my grandparents, managed to pick up a smattering of ASL and fingerspelling and are able to converse more or less successfully with their grandparents. My wife also became adept in the basic signs and fingerspelling, and manages to hold her own, calling on me from time to time to help her out. Mom has kept her vivacity and her health to this day, but Aunt Eleanor lives in the nursing home in Upper Sandusky, and my parents and my Aunt Jean devote themselves to visiting and looking in on her as their own health allows. Aunt Dorothy died on September 11, 2002.

In the spring of 1980, Mom is about to turn sixty-two, and she, Dad, and I talked about her taking early retirement. Mom has worked since 1954 at that same highly stressful, physically demanding job, pressing shirts. She is on her feet all day long, moving rapidly among three presses, constantly having to coordinate her movements to be certain the shirts come out absolutely wrinkle-free. Today, those old presses are now obsolete simply because they require so much skill and energy to operate. She is paid piecework, or by the shirt, so she has to work fast to make a decent wage for herself and for her assistant, whose paycheck also depends on Mom's speed at the presses. Finally, she confesses to being fatigued, burned out, and ready to pack it in. She turns to me and says, "I want you to go with me to the Social Security office and help me apply." Her request gives me quite a sense of déjà vu. Thirty years earlier, I would have cringed; now, I'm more than willing. I explain to her the financial advantages and disadvantages of retiring early, and she decides that it is time.

We drive to the Social Security office, her application is processed without a hitch, and I am happy to have been able to help. The experience makes me realize how much I have matured, how I have been able to conquer the demons of shyness and fear that beset me as a young boy when I was called on to play the part of an adult. I realize how much I had immersed myself in that world of need that bound me to my parents and how much I still miss it.

Life is full of ironies. My mother, who was always the "handi-capped," impetuous, wayward daughter and poor relation, has had the good life in the end, faring better in the long run than her three sisters, widowed and broken in health, of whom her favorite, Dorothy, is no longer with us. My Uncle Lester, Dad's brother, spent the last months of his life in a rest home, a victim of the senility that claimed his mother, Grandma Amy. He died in July 2002. In spite of nagging health problems, my dad remains as sharp as ever.

With that inevitable separation between my parents and me when I went off to college, I lost a precious part of my life, my association with Deaf culture. I have always missed their Deaf friends, the Silent Club, the get-togethers. Now, most of their friends are gone and have been replaced by a more savvy, better educated group of Deaf people, generationally distant from my parents and from me. When I talk with these Deaf people, I marvel at all they have achieved, but sometimes when I encounter that generational disdain that they feel for Deaf members of my parents' generation, I am tempted to say to them (and I have no right to say it), "You just don't understand what it was like. You don't understand."

Most of all, I miss the use of sign language. Over the years, I have seen my skills decline. My parents never did fully immerse us in ASL and depended on a combination of oral methods and signing, a kind of home signing, probably to protect their privacy and because their Hearing families told them that ASL would stunt the language development of their children. As a result, my communication with my parents always has an aura of the infantile about it, and when I talk to them, I feel as if I have become a little boy, speaking to my parents in a kind of child language. I was always envious of the ASL skills of many of my CODA friends because they were much more at home using signs with their parents than any of us Miller kids were. Much as I wanted to participate in the Deaf community, I

Mom, Dad, and Bob at their home, Defiance, Ohio, 1995.

knew I was an outsider and would remain so. I also believe my parents harbored a degree of shame over their Deafness, which was reinforced by their Hearing families—as if somehow it were a punishment for some deep family sin—and they did what they could to isolate their children from it. They wanted their children to succeed, and they knew the path to success lay in the Hearing world.

The year is 1998. My youngest brother, John, at fifty-one, has had an aneurysm burst near his brain stem. He lives about fifteen miles from my parents' home, in the town of Continental. After being taken to Defiance Hospital, he is transferred to a hospital in Fort Wayne, Indiana, then immediately to Methodist Hospital in Indianapolis, which is about two hours away from my home in Louisville, so as soon as I can, I drive up to see him.

As the oldest in the family, it shocks me to see my youngest brother come so near death. He is semicomatose, but he is alive. My mother, my brother Art, and John's wife, Essie, are all there. I tell them I plan to come up in a few days to see him again, and we try to schedule my next visit on a day when they won't be there because they are making the six-hour, round-trip drive from Defiance almost daily.

During my next visit, I am alone with him in the special neurological care unit, after he's gained consciousness and some use of his limbs. He is sedated and is resting in a high-tech version of a La-Z-Boy™ recliner, a piece of furniture that is standard decor in almost every small-town home in Ohio. Tubes wind every which way, and a ghastly look-ing shunt protrudes from his forehead. Because he is still on a ventilator, he is unable to talk, but he recognizes me, and he has some limited use of his hands and arms.

As if it were second nature to him, he begins signing to me, and we manage to carry on a conversation. I see him tiring, so I tell him I have to go, and as I bend over to give him a light hug and a kiss, he lifts his arms. Tubes clatter and flap dangerously about, but he manages to cross his forearms, with his fists clenched, over his chest in an embrace, and then points his finger at me, in the traditional ASL sign for "I love you," not the clichéd, extended-thumb-and-two-fingers sign that has become so popular today. I am deeply moved by this expression of affection from my brother, whom I seldom see and am not really close to, but then I realize that it has special meaning because he signed to me. The signing is everything and means more to me than the spoken words.

John Adam Miller died July 29, 2002.

John's funeral is held in Pleasant View Missionary Baptist Church, in Junction, not far from the Junction Cemetery. He is buried in the

*new Riverview Memory Gardens, north of Defiance, where my parents
will also be buried. At the funeral, the preacher notes the sizeable Deaf
attendance and also the presence of the interpreter, my parents' minister,
and remarks that, when we all meet in heaven, the Deaf people will be
cured and we'll all be able to talk together and hear one another. After
the service, I say to Mom and Dad that when we go to heaven maybe
we'll all be Deaf, and we'll hear in a new, a special way. At first, they
are a little uncomfortable with their oldest son's impertinence on the day
of his brother's funeral, but then they nod their heads, smile, and move
their fists in the sign for YES.*

> "Heard melodies are sweet, but those unheard
> Are sweeter; therefore, ye soft pipes, play on;
> Not to the sensual ear, but, more endear'd,
> Pipe to the spirit ditties of no tone."
>
> —*John Keats*, "Ode on a Grecian Urn"

Afterword

Long before Lionel Trilling dubbed Robert Frost the "Poet of Terror," Frost himself is said to have described childhood as the "Age of Terror." The point behind Frost's remarkable insight is that what he said is true of all our childhoods regardless of whether they are happy, troubled, or victimized by abuse. In fact, for most of us, "happy childhood" may be something of an oxymoron. As children, all of us lived in the shadow of terrifying possibilities, beleaguered by a sense of helplessness and a fear of what we did not know. My childhood and adolescence were unique only because, as the Hearing child of Deaf parents, I had certain responsibilities. I had to cope with the stresses that came from having to assume an unusual role—that of an adult—while I was still very much a child and, I confess, a child not well suited to play that role.

In other ways, I was an ordinary kid and lived a life not much different from those of my boyhood pals. Like my father, I was shy and introverted, and underneath my bluster, I'm still that shy little boy. Hearing people attributed my shyness to being raised by Deaf parents, assuming that somehow my upbringing was stunting me emotionally, but nothing could have been further from the truth. In fact, the example of my parents is what taught me to have confidence and self-respect, and to them, I am grateful for those lessons.

Writing this book was painful, more so than I expected, but also liberating. As one who has avoided any kind of therapy or counseling, although I am sure I could have benefited from both, I was surprised at every turn in the road by revelations that came to me as I thought more intensely than I ever had before about those early days with my parents. Until these last few years, I had created a kind of happy fiction about it—a Horatio Alger story in which I overcame obstacles and my parents strove faultlessly against overwhelming prejudice as they provided me and my three brothers with flawless parenting.

This creation, of course, was far from true. I believed I had had a normal, even somewhat privileged childhood, and I thought I could have been a better boy and a better son. Fortunately, most children live the lives they have been given without questioning anything and are not aware of the shortcomings of their parents until they have grown up and developed some perspective on the adult world. I certainly followed that progression and believed I had lived through a "normal" childhood when, actually, I had not. In contrast to other CODAs who have left us records of their lives with Deaf parents, most notably Lou Ann Walker and Lennard Davis, my life was complicated further by the presence in the household of my Hearing grandparents, and I was deeply conflicted about my responses to the pressures that not only my Deaf parents but also my Hearing grand-parents put on me.

Many of my opinions and feelings do not reflect those of my brothers, but although we each had our different experiences at home, whatever shortcomings we thought our parents may have possessed, we all agree they loved us and did their best for us. My brother Dick found reading an earlier draft of this book a revelation because he was much closer to my situation than either Art or John, whose family experiences were very different because my parents were settled in their lifelong occupations and financially stable when they were growing up. Art found that this memoir was a description of a family he would be hard put to recognize. Unfortunately, John did not live to see a copy of the book.

The Deaf world my parents lived in was far more insulated from the Hearing world than it is today, and Deaf people of that genera-tion were at a serious disadvantage in finding their roles in mainstream society. By today's standards for Deaf people, my parents were poorly educated and had to overcome many prejudices against them. Because of their handicap, their language deprivation, and their unusual method of communication, they were often looked on as mentally defective, indeed, almost alien. They had no Americans with Disabilities Act to protect them; they had only their courage and determination and the good will of a few corporations and businesses that were willing to employ them.

Often, as my parents engaged their friends in lively signing con-versation, I felt a barrier go up between the world I lived in and the one they lived in, as if my parents had crossed a divide that I could not cross. Recently, I relived that experience at my parents' sixty-fifth wedding anniversary where, to my great delight, I reunited with Deaf friends I had not seen in more than fifty years. As the afternoon wore on and as we had exhausted our news of one another and I had also exhausted my limited signing skills, my brothers and I and our families found ourselves isolated with the small Hearing group at the party, while the Deaf group talked on and on. Yet quite often, for example, over dinner when we, their Hearing family, carry on our conversations, I can see the pain behind my parents' quizzical faces as they try to ravel out what we might be talking about. We always mean to include them, but often, the flow gets to be so lively that we leave them behind—thoughtless and rude, yes, but over time, inevitable. In the end, I suppose this part of my life is as much about separation as it is about inclusion, and like Matthew Arnold's pilgrim to the Grand Chartreuse, I have spent a great deal of my life wandering between these two worlds.

Life for Deaf people today continues to be a challenge. The disappearance of blue-collar jobs and the demand for highly trained workers have put Deaf people at a serious disadvantage in the labor market. Since my parents' days as schoolchildren, many advances have occurred in education for and attitudes about Deaf children. In fact, people today have difficulty recalling a time when the public generally considered education of Deaf children a wasted effort and often relegated them to poorly funded, poorly managed, and philosophically and educationally misguided institutions. They separated children from their homes at an age when they needed the support of parents and siblings, as my mother and father were separated from theirs and suffered because of that breach. And they looked after the children until either they graduated or they reached the age at which they could no longer be kept in school.

From another perspective, however, my parents in some ways benefited from their close association with their peers at school. Of the choices available to them at that time—life at home with parents who were not prepared to raise a deaf child or life in an institution that made at least an effort to meet their needs—the institution was often the better option.

But inevitably, this institutional upbringing had a price, and Deaf people paid it along with their children, the CODAs (children of Deaf adults) of my generation, who also ended up paying a part of it. In the institutions, staff members maintained a strict, puritanical discipline among the children, many of whom were poorly socialized because they had been neglected at home, and my parents were prone to apply those same measures to their children. My parents were brought up on a regimen of stern morality that often was not clearly explained, corporal punishment, hard physical labor at janitorial and other duties in the school, wholesome but simple food, carefully regulated activities that did not allow for much exploration or choice, and rigorous study habits. Naturally, this kind of life shaped my parents' attitudes toward parenting and toward their children. Yet, like many Deaf people, my parents would not exchange their institutional experience for any other and are skeptical of "mainstreaming," the educational philosophy that advocates keeping deaf children in their family settings and in regular school programs.

As a parent now myself, I often have difficulty judging the parenting I received because I have become keenly aware that all parents fail at it to some degree. As I wrote this book, I thought frequently of my three daughters and what they might write about me as a father. As Hamlet says, if we all got what we deserved, who of us would escape whipping? By any standard, my parents were good parents of Hearing children. In so many ways, they were so much more successful than their parents who had failed in many ways because they were so ignorant of the nature of Deafness. Their parents' ignorance of ASL was even more damaging; Deaf oralist professionals had discouraged them from learning ASL and, hence, from being able to communicate in a complex, sophisticated manner with their children. If their parents had known as much about the Deaf world as my parents eventually knew about the Hearing world, things would have been very different for them all.

Nevertheless, even though both my mom and dad were poorly prepared for parenthood, they made a success of it against enormous difficulties, as did their Deaf friends. Institutionalization left its mark on their parenting habits, as I tried to show in this book, and one can only hope that Deaf education today, especially in Deaf residential schools, helps young Deaf women and men face the practicalities of everyday living, especially parenting. In the end, Mom and Dad made it through the challenges and proved to be caring parents. They were devoted to their boys, and my brothers and I are the beneficiaries of their care and their love.